Assessing Writing

Explorations in Language Study

Explorations in Language Study
General Editors
Peter Doughty   Geoffrey Thornton

ASSESSING WRITING: PRINCIPLES AND PRACTICE OF MARKING WRITTEN ENGLISH

Peter Gannon

EDWARD ARNOLD

© Peter Gannon 1985

First published in Great Britain 1985 by
Edward Arnold (Publishers) Ltd, 41 Bedford Square, London WC1B 3DQ

Edward Arnold (Australia) Pty Ltd, 80 Waverley Road, Caulfield East,
Victoria 3145, Australia

Edward Arnold, 300 North Charles Street, Baltimore, Maryland 21201, U.S.A.

British Library Cataloguing in Publication Data

Gannon, Peter
　　Assessing writing: principles and practice
　　of marking written English. ——(Explorations
　　in language study)
　　1. English language —— Rhetoric —— Study and
　　teaching　2. Grading and marking (Students)
　　I. Title　II. Series
　　808′.042′071　　LB1631

　　ISBN 0-7131-6439-5

Text set in 11/12pt Baskerville
by Colset Private Limited, Singapore
Printed and bound by Richard Clay (The Chaucer Press) Ltd,
Bungay, Suffolk

Contents

Acknowledgements

I should like to acknowledge the suggestions and help provided in the writing of this book by my friends and colleagues, especially Sally Twite, Geoffrey Thornton and Sarah Barrett. A special kind of thanks must go to my family, whose forebearance should be gratefully admitted, as should that of every writer's family.

Peter Gannon

General introduction

In the course of our efforts to develop a linguistic focus for work in English language, which was published as *Language in Use*, we came to realize the extent of the growing interest in what we would call a linguistic approach to language. Lecturers in Colleges and Departments of Education see the relevance of such an approach in the education of teachers. Many teachers in schools and in Colleges of Further Education recognize that 'educational failure is primarily *linguistic* failure', and are turning to linguistic science for some kind of exploration and practical guidance. Many of those now exploring the problems of relationships, community or society, from a sociological or psychological point of view wish to make use of a linguistic approach to the language in so far as it is relevant to these problems.

We were conscious of the wide divergence between the aims of the linguist, primarily interested in describing language as a system for organizing 'meanings', and the needs of those who now wanted to gain access to the insights that resulted from that interest. In particular, we were aware of the wide gap that separated the literature of academic linguistics from the majority of those who wished to find out what linguistic science might have to say about language and the use of language.

Out of this experience emerged our own view of that much-used term, 'language study', developed initially in the chapters of *Exploring language*, and now given expression in this series. Language study is not a subject, but a process, which is why the series is called *Explorations in Language Study*. Each exploration is focused upon a meeting point between the insights of linguistic science, often in conjunction with other social sciences, and the linguistic questions raised by the study of a particular aspect of individual behaviour or human society.

The volumes in the series have a particular relevance to the role of language in teaching and learning. The editors intend that they should make a basic contribution to the literature of language study, doing justice equally to the findings of the academic disciplines involved and the practical needs of those who now want to take a linguistic view of their own particular problems of language and the use of language.

Peter Doughty
Geoffrey Thornton

Introduction

It is in the nature of teaching to make judgements; to decide whether one piece of work is better than another, whether a pupil is developing satisfactorily in terms of acquiring understanding and knowledge, whether new knowledge is being satisfactorily introduced and explained, and so on. This applies whether we are speaking of chemistry or cricket, biology or baseball, Russian or writing. The kind of judgements made by teachers on the quality of children's writing is one of the most important elements of children's education. Writing is central to almost every activity in the educational system. But in most of the classrooms of our schools, a paradox persists: while enormous quantities of writing are produced by pupils, demanding millions of pupil hours, and while most of it is read and marked by teachers, there is a constant dissatisfaction with both the quality of much that is produced and with the efficacy of many of the marking procedures used. The previous volume in this series, *Teaching writing*, by Geoffrey Thornton, addressed the first of those two issues: the quality of writing produced, its development, and those aspects of teaching and learning which might facilitate the achieving of higher standards in writing performance. This volume addresses the second of those issues: the process of responding to and making judgements about what is produced by pupils, especially in English lessons. There is, of course, no way of prescribing easy solutions to any problem in education. It would be impertinent of the present writer to imply that definitive answers are to be found in this short contribution to the lengthy and continuing consideration of how best to respond to children's writing. But some of the suggestions made may be of some use to some teachers.

In order to clear away some of the misconceptions abounding

with regard to what teachers are asking for when they set writing tasks, chapter 1 deals with some of the areas to be cleared; and in chapter 2, comment is made on some of the relationships between speech and writing, and of both to language. Chapters 3 and 4 become less discursive, and a little more detailed, and, for clarity's sake, each of these chapters concludes with a summary of its contents. The fifth chapter displays in brief an application of the notions previously considered, while the sixth mentions some of the implications for teaching.

Some of the assumptions underlying what is said below are made explicit. Others are not. It is for readers to decide whether what is written here matches their own views on the nature and process of education, on the function of schools, on the purposes of writing, and on the relevance to their own needs and concerns of a more systematic view of marking than is generally apparent in schools.

1
Marking, correcting and assessing

As mentioned in the introduction, one of the most popular volumes in this series is called *Teaching writing* by Geoffrey Thornton (1980). In that work, chapters 5 and 6 contain a large number of helpful suggestions about how to respond to writing in school. Do we need a separate book on *assessing* writing, when those who deal with writing *development* are constantly referring to response and assessment, as they are? It may to some people seem strange, or even wrong, to find assessment being treated separately from teaching. After all, assessment is part of teaching. When we mark a collection of stories from our third-year junior class or a set of essays from our fifth-year O-level class, it is all part of the teaching task. Teachers, especially English teachers, spend many hours grading classwork, correcting those tiresome errors which crop up again and again (*their/there, could have/could of*, and so on), or simply commenting on a piece of homework well done. Do we really need to do more than agree about a few conventional abbreviations — 'Sp' for 'spelling error', 'n.p.' for 'new paragraph', and so on? I think we do, and that opinion, based on experience, is the *raison d'être* of this book.

In the paragraph you have just read, there are six words or phrases which have been used to refer to aspects of what I shall call assessment. Consider the list: 'respond to', 'assessing', 'mark', 'grading', 'correcting' 'commenting on'. Is there any difference between correcting and assessing, or between responding to a piece of work and marking it? The commonest term of all is 'marking'. Teachers mark books. It is a law of pedagogy. It is, moreover, a law which is almost everywhere strictly observed within the education system. When the law is disregarded, it attracts disapproval from head teachers, parents and others. This point is not a flippant one.

In most secondary schools, an averagely conscientious teacher of English may expect in the course of a year to spend between 200 and 400 hours marking pupils' writing. That amounts to 25 to 50 full working days in addition to days spent teaching in the classroom. Between five and ten extra weeks a year, then, are being worked by teachers; and those five to 10 weeks are often largely wasted, since frequently little perceptible improvement occurs in levels of performance from one term to the next. How to avoid the waste is our theme.

Here a word on terminology may not come amiss. Several writers have commented upon the connotations of the term 'marking'. In *The resources of classroom language* (Richmond 1982, 221), John Richmond refers to 'the complete lack of coordination on what is still meanly called "marking". The economistic nature of schooling was never better sketched than in that all-pervading little word.' In *Teaching writing*, Geoffrey Thornton suggests that we should abandon the term 'marking' altogether (Thornton 1980, 38). I propose to continue using the term, mainly because it is part of our educational vocabulary, and we all know to what it refers even though we may have different perceptions of what is involved. It is no slur upon the conscientiousness of teachers to refer to their wasting time. Consider the piece of work reproduced opposite, written by a pupil in the top class of a junior school, complete with the teacher's marking.

Before we look in detail at the child's composition, what is the immediate impression given by the teacher's response as shown by the symbols and comment? There are 20 separate features 'marked' in this piece of nine lines, and it is almost certain that those 20 'marks' on the page add up to a response which is so overwhelming that it will probably be ignored by the writer. The message being conveyed by the teacher is likely to be equivalent to little more than: 'You have made a large number of errors.' The commendation at the end will be received in one of two ways. Either it will be isolated by the child and received independently of all the red marks preceding it, or its sense will be vitiated by the sheer quantity of previous marking. In either case the teacher's effort has been wasted. If the experienced pupil (and he *is* experienced, after nearly seven years at school) simply isolates the comment and grade, he is bound to be complacent. Who would not be, with 70 per cent and a 'well done'? If the pupil is overcome by quantities of red ink, then the whole exercise is put to the back of the mind. This amounts to waste.

It is worth considering in a little more detail the nature of this marking exercise, because it is typical of what is going on all over the country in hundreds of schools. The implications are both pedagogic and linguistic. First, the marking is literally incomprehensible. How does a piece of nine lines that has 20 errors receive a mark of seven out of ten? Surely the implication is either that the errors are not important enough to warrant more than a deduction of three marks, especially in view of the 'Well done' at the end, or that the errors *are* important but the teacher is bestowing false praise.

Now, it is of course very important that teachers should avoid the deadly effect of negative marking. In the survey of aspects of the secondary curriculum carried out by HM Inspectorate in 1975-78 there is, in chapter 6, a stark illustration of how negative marking persists (DES 1979, 89):

13

The failure to regard writing as part of the learning process was responsible for marking which was not only at times haphazard, casual or inconsistent, but at other times negative, censorious and possibly counterproductive. This record of the work of a fifth-year pupil may be cited. Her written work had been selected by the school as that of a very able pupil, and clearly demonstrated that she was. A series of essays in English over a term earned this total sequence of comments in the page margins and at the end of compositions;

— Not thought out
— Full stops and caps not clearly written
— Errors of fact
— You write a letter as briefly as possible
— Needs more careful thought
— Not developed
— Padding
— You have not thought this out sufficiently
— Is this all?
— Weak
— Not what you were told to do
— Keep it clear, concise and simple
— Spoilt by carelessness
— Tenses
— Keep it clear, concise and simple
— Argument poor
— Repetition
— Poorly expressed
— Meaningless
— Rubbish
— Last paragraph muddled
— Last paragraph shows thought.

The fact that the girl had continued to write at all in the face of such bilious comment is, one might suppose, a manifestation of ability.

In that paragraph we have a depressing condensation of teaching practices that are almost certainly bound to be counterproductive. It may be that in the five years since the recording of that kind of censoriousness, practice has changed a little, and teachers are now more warmly praising in their comments. But if so, it is still no more productive in raising levels of performance, since marking of written work is still uneven, idiosyncratic, and for the most part confined to proof-reading at a very superficial level.

This is illustrated in the 'nightmare' text shown on p. 13. One of the most interesting features has passed quite unremarked by the teacher. In line 7, the pupil has written:

> The unicorn was kicking and the headless horse was whipping and laughing

Now that doesn't make much sense. Presumably, the pupil meant to write:

> The unicorn was kicking and the headless horseman was whipping it and laughing

(Let us leave aside for the moment the impossibility of being able to laugh without a head.)

The crucial omission of the pronoun *it* has escaped the teacher's notice because it occurs in the only line which has no spelling and punctuation errors. Apart from an alteration to the sentence structure in line 4, all the marks are concerned with either spelling or punctuation. Perhaps, however, the teacher noticed the faulty structure in line 7 but chose not to comment, feeling that there was sufficient quality in the piece to justify overlooking that particular point. If so, it is a pity, because it might have been better to have commented *only* on that, and to have ignored many of the other points. For this piece by an 11-year-old has some powerful features and it is worth spending a little longer in explicitly acknowledging them.

The title is *The nightmare* and the first sentence immediately achieves the sense of dread we associate with a bad dream. It does so in two ways. First, the use of the impersonal *it* avoids precision and reinforces bewilderment. We do not know whether the thing that is running is human or monstrous. Second, the physical displacement felt in dreams is captured by the deliberate contradiction of *running to* and *moving away*. Not until line 4 do we have the specifying phrase *headless Horseman*. The dream quality is suddenly reinforced in lines 5 and 6 when we read *it was riding around the moon*. While there is a hint of remembered fairytales in *the clock struck midnight* (Cinderella, perhaps?) the rhythm of the last two lines maintains the strange ritual of dreams. So in both the content and the organization of the material in this strange little piece, there is a strong intuitive 'shaping' instinct at work. Both the grammar and the orthography are faulty, although only the latter has been noted by the teacher, whose intuition, in awarding 7 out of 10 and in admitting to the deliberately frightening quality of the writing, was almost certainly seizing on the overall effect rather than on the shaky spelling. But in that case, what was the purpose of the marking exercise?

This brings us to the question — why do we mark writing? That very question was put to about 40 teachers on a residential course on language development. All the teachers replied, and the answers made interesting reading. They varied from the innocently pragmatic 'the head/head of department/parent expects it' to the thoughtful 'to enable the child to improve his writing abilities and so narrow the gap between his oral fluency and his hesitation in writing'. Between these two very different responses was a collection of more or less benevolent aspirations, eg. 'to encourage the child', 'to see if the child is learning what he has been taught', 'to show the child that teachers take notice of what he does at school'. Only one entirely circular proposition was advanced, and that, I am sure, more in innocence than cynicism — 'to fill up the mark book'! Later, towards the end of the same course, another question was put: 'How do you mark writing?' This time only 17 teachers replied. Of the 17 responses, 10 were evasive — 'it depends on what has been set' or 'it depends which group it is — and the other 7 were remarkably similar, typified by one which read, 'I look for the important mistakes and then make a general comment'.

All those teacher comments quoted show three things. First, the ten 'evasive' responses were not avoiding a reply. They were almost certainly an expression of a very proper view that it is dangerous to try to assess a piece of writing out of context, ie. without knowing the child, the nature of the task, its origins or its purposes. If so, that is entirely to be welcomed and we shall return to that aspect later (see pp. 31–3); next, there is from the variety of response a good deal of confusion about the purposes of marking; third, there is also a considerable measure of vagueness about appropriateness of methods. Rarely was there any mention of selectivity about what was to be marked, and in only a very few responses was there any indication that for practical teaching purposes it is frequently necessary to disregard many features of writing and to concentrate on only one or a few at a time.

The confusion referred to reflects, perhaps, an uncertainty about the relationship of *form* with *function*. The effectiveness of writing is judged by readers in the world outside school pragmatically, in terms of what is communicated, of its value to the reader, and of the reader's perception of how closely *what* is being communicated relates to *how* it is being communicated, i.e. in terms of how the content and function relate to the form. Sometimes the form is quite unimportant, as in a hastily written note to a close friend, in which the informational content overrides all other considerations. In a certain kind of lyric poem, on the other hand, the conceptual content may be minimal, but the form all-important. The relationship between form and function is the basis for a number of frameworks for categorizing writing; perhaps that best known to most teachers is the spectrum of writing types denoted by the terms 'transactional — expressive — poetic', devised by James Britton (see Britton 1970), mentioned in the Bullock Report (see DES 1975) and by a Schools Council Project (see, for example, Mallet and Newsome 1977, 132−8). Much has been written about that particular framework; and while there is no doubt that many English teachers have found it to be of general use, it has several disadvantages (see Gannon and Czerniewska 1980, 191).

To return to the main point — in most cases, there is overlap between form and function, the 'how' and the 'why'. Most readers make generalized judgements, without distinguishing the 'how' from the 'why'. When we read a newspaper article, or a chapter of a novel, we do not, in most cases, separate considerations of form from those of content. We read a piece and decide whether it is well or ill written; and usually only later, if it strikes us as meriting closer attention, do we pay conscious attention to specific features such as the sentence structure or the sequence of thoughts. This is recognized, at least implicitly, by most teachers when they talk of 'impression marking'. Impression marking should not be lightly dismissed, or indeed dismissed at all. There is a substantial amount of research which shows a high correlation between the results of impression marking of experienced teachers and the results obtained from a number of analytic marking schemes. The intuition of a teacher who has been exposed to thousands of scripts of different kinds from pupils of different ages and abilities is a powerful instrument of assessment. It is when we are faced with specific features, however, that intuition alone will not suffice. When we come across such examples as

If someone said I will be helpful and was he was strong (11-year-old)

or

> She asked some others to and sit down on the near her desk there
> did some number (11-year-old)

We need to do more than say 'the first example is better than the second' or 'the second is pretty poor stuff'. We may, of course, at a first reading of any writing at all, talk to ourselves in such an informal manner. Who has not had the experience of reading or hearing a favourite passage from, say, Shakespeare, and saying 'Good stuff, this!'? But we do not fool ourselves into believing that that crude, if silent, informality constitutes valid literary criticism. It may well be a precursor to critical commentary, just as when we say to ourselves of a child's page, 'not very good', that may well be the prelude to some very helpful, detailed and sympathetic response, since we wish to help the child to write better than he or she does.

In order to arrive at some sensible and useable framework of assessment, certain prerequisites have to be fulfilled. We need to have in mind some important facts about the nature of language and in particular the English language; similarly we need to know some important facts about the nature of writing in general and English writing in particular; and we also need to have some clear notions about such matters as reasonable expectations for different age groups. Only then can we go on to devise a useable framework and a means of recording the progress made by pupils. All these concerns are the matter of this book. Chapter 2 deals with a number of things we need to know about language and the writing system. Chapter 3 is concerned with the purposes of writing, while chapters 4 and 5 outline an approach towards marking pupils' written work which takes into account the material discussed in earlier chapters, and illustrates it with examples. A final chapter mentions some implications for implementing such an approach in the normal curriculum.

Writing is, and for a long time will continue to be, the chief skill by which school children will manage to achieve success, or not, within our education system. Some pupils will succeed and some will fail, as they do now. No more needs to be said about the education system itself, since this book is neither a political nor a sociological tract. The central point is that if teachers can sharpen and refine their methods of assessing and responding to children's efforts as they practise their writing skills, then perhaps more

18

children might write better than many now do by the time they leave school at the age of 16. More importantly, we may see more of a progression through the secondary years of schooling than at present seems to exist. One of the more worrying findings of the Assessment of Performance Unit is that there is too little development evident between the ages of 11 and 16 (see DES 1984).

2
Language, speech and writing

It may seem self-evident that if one wishes to assess the value of something, one first needs to know what that something is. As far as writing is concerned, it is not at all obvious just what is being judged. Are we considering how well the marks on paper correspond to the orthographic conventions in use, how sensitively words have been chosen, how sentences have been formed, how sentences hang together, how accurately what is being written reflects what we think the writer intended, how original the content seems to be, how the rhythm of the language used relates to the content, how far the intended reader has been considered in the writing — i.e. how friendly, hostile, formal, informal, clear, consistent the style may be — or just how attractive it all looks on paper? We could go on for pages with similar questions and still not exhaust the list of features for which we may at one time or another be searching in a piece of writing.

When we consider all these questions, saying what writing is becomes a more complex matter than at first it may have seemed. To the very young, it is very simple. A week before writing the sentence now being read, I asked a seven-year-old child the question, 'What is writing?' The reply came without hesitation: 'It's when you say on paper what you think.' For that seven-year-old, saying and thinking and writing were all connected. They are connected, of course, but not in such a direct and simple way as may be thought.

All natural languages are spoken. By 'natural language' I mean a language which is used by a group or groups of human beings, but which has not been artificially devised, as, for example, Esperanto. (There is no need, for present purposes, to become involved in deciding what the difference is between a language and a dialect.) No-one has been able accurately to count the total number of languages in the world, but most linguists agree that there are between 4000 and 5000. Some are spoken by only a few hundred individuals, others (like English) by hundreds of millions. But the fact remains that all are spoken. However, only a minority of languages are written (see A. Brookes and R. Hudson in Carter 1982); and of that minority, few have a standardized written form. English happens to be one of that number of languages that has a written and standardized form.

This is not the place to indulge in comment upon that most fascinating of topics the history of the English language. But it is important to have in mind the fact that the language, in both spoken and written forms, has a long history. For writing is not merely 'speech written down'; there is a speech system and a writing system, and they have diverged considerably over the years, in systematic but different ways. In a most useful recent book on teaching the spoken language, Gillian Brown (Brown and Yule 1983) has some important things to note about the differences between speech and writing, as well as pointing out that these differences may be determined by the *functions* of each. Obviously we have no access to the way human beings spoke thousands of years ago, though we do know how some of them wrote. From the earliest writing extant, it seems that the function of written language had a very practical nature. Gillian Brown (Brown and Yule 1983, 10), quoting J. Goody (1977) mentions that a basic purpose of writing, historically speaking, was to record facts about aspects of society which would cause confusion if left unrecorded. In a preelectronic era, writing fulfilled a function of which speech was incapable.

We shall return later to the functions of speech and writing; here it is important merely to stress the fact that writing is not just 'speech written down', as the seven-year-old seemed to think. The truth of this is easily demonstrated by reading a transcription of actual speech. In Brown and Yule 1983, there is a transcription (pp. 11−12) of speech occurring during a discussion among four adults, mentioning another couple who visit a particular area of the country each year (the plus sign marks a pause):

A: you know but erm + they used to go out in erm August + they used to come + you know the lovely sunsets you get + at that time and
B: oh yes

C: there's a nice new postcard a nice − well I don't know how new it is + it's been a while since I've been here + of a sunset + a new one +

A: oh that's a lovely one isn't it

D: yes yes it was in one of the + calendars

A: yes that was last year's calendar it was on

D: was it last year's it was on + it was John Forgan who took that one

A: yes it's really lovely + this year's erm + the Andersons' house at Lenimore's in it + at erm Thunderguy I should say

D: they've sold their house

A: yes + the Andersons

B: oh have they

A: yes yes + erm + they weren't down last year at all

Now, from the above, several things are clear. First, the utterances of the speakers are not structured in ways we associate with writing. How would you mark the first three utterances, if they were handed to you as a piece of writing? The chances are that you would have something to say about the sentence structure. Then, there is no single identifiable topic in the above quotation. Is the conversation about postcards, or calenders, or the Andersons? Next, we might notice that there is a good deal of repetition of certain kinds of words or phrases − the word *yes* occurs eight times. And this stretch of speech could not have occurred without four participants simultaneously participating in the 'speech event'. Now, none of these features normally occurs in most kinds of writing, and if they did, a teacher would regard them as faults − poor structure, poor organization of material, repetition, getting someone else to produce part of what should be individual work, etc. But of course we do not assess speech by the same criteria as we do writing.

Other writers have dwelt upon the differences between speech and writing (see especially Thornton 1980 and Stubbs 1980) and we do not need to list the differences here; we do need to stress that the writing system of English is different from the speech system. When children use terms such as 'language', 'speech' and 'writing', they tend to use them interchangeably. But the relationships among the three terms are not of the same kind. Obviously, in informal conversation, no harm comes from ignoring the differences, but it is important for us to recognize them. So the relationships between language, writing and speech in English are not, as for our seven-year-old:

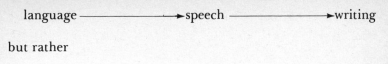

but rather

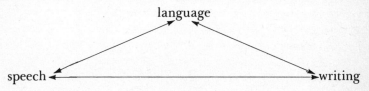

There are, as the double-headed arrow between 'speech' and 'writing' indicates, relationships between the two, but they are different systems, and each has its own 'rules' and conventions. They may overlap, but they are not identical. It is implied, in the second figure, that language is somehow a more general term than either speech or writing; indeed, it must be so, since a person speaking in English and a person writing in English are both drawing upon the resources of the same language, even though each is using a rather different system. Language is here used to refer to the abstract structures and relationships within what we call English, which it is the job of the linguist to describe. A brief set of comments on each of the three terms may now be useful, in the interests of clarity later.

Language

1 A language is a system of communication by vocal sounds within a group of human beings who use those sounds to convey meanings. It may or may not have a set of conventional, visible, material signs, called a writing system.

2 Any language can be described in terms of units − for example, sentences, or words, or even units smaller than the word. The word *kicked* may be thought of as two units, *kick* + *ed*, where *ed* carries the meaning 'past tense'.

3 Some units have form but no meaning. For example, the *b* in *ball* has form, which can be described in terms of its sound features, but it has no meaning by itself. Other units have both form and meaning, e.g. *ball* is a unit we call a word; its form can be described in terms of its acoustic or articulatory properties, syllabic structure, and so on, while its meaning can be described with reference to its significance in referring to some aspect of the world

(whether that be a round object, or a grand, formal dance, or whatever).

4 The units of a language form larger units in predictable ways — e.g. the four words *kicked*, *he*, *ball*, *the* can be reordered into three elements — *he*, *kicked*, *the ball*, among which *the ball* may be described as the object of the sentence *he kicked the ball*. The term 'sentence' itself refers to an even larger unit. Larger units are all composed of smaller units or units which are of equivalent 'size'.

5 A formal description of the way units of a language interrelate in systematic ways is a grammar. The generalized statements which describe the relationships are called 'rules'. They are descriptive statements, not prescriptive laws.

Speech

1 Speech is what renders concrete language (itself an abstract system) *in all natural languages*.

2 Speech is usually an interactional process. That is, it consists of a face-to-face exchange between or among two or more inter-locutors. Sometimes, as in a lecture, or when speaking to oneself, it is less interactional than is normally the case.

3 Speech is usually accompanied by nonlinguistic features of behaviour, such as facial expression, or gesture, both to convey meanings and, on the part of the hearer(s), to signal reactions to the behaviour of the speaker(s).

4 Speech occurs in time and is usually modified as it occurs to take account of the listener's reactions. For example, if you see that your hearer is looking puzzled, you may repeat what you have said, in a different way; you will modify what you are saying *as you are saying it*, in order to satisfy yourself that the meaning is being clearly conveyed.

5 Speech usually contains a fair amount of repetition and redund-ancy, since human beings have limited attention spans and limited short-term memories (try repeating an eight-digit number after only one hearing). The redundancy is therefore natural and neces-sary, and not a mark of inefficiency.

6 Because of 1-5 above, speech has typical systematic features which are different from those of writing. These differences are manifested at different levels of complexity — at the level of indi-vidual speech sounds, at word, clause, and sentence level, and in the ways in which sentences and sets of sentences interrelate.

7 There are also significant correspondences between speech and writing. For example, there are regularities in the rise and fall of the voice (intonation) which are in part paralleled by the punctuation conventions of writing.

Writing

1 Writing is a way of realizing language in those communities which have acquired a writing system. It is characterized by its use of visible signs systematically ordered. In English it is an alphabetic system, in which letters and groups of letters correspond in fairly regular ways to the vocal sounds of speech. The systems may be alphabetic, as in most European languages, or syllabic, as in Japanese, or 'logographic' (in which characters relate to the smallest units of meaning), as in Chinese. Most languages use systems which are predominantly one of the three types mentioned.

2 Writing is usually an individual process. That is, a writer makes marks on a surface, which will be looked at by someone else later. A piece of writing constitutes a visible product which remains, while it is being read, unaltered. It is thus different from speech, which is modified as it occurs.

3 A writer has to consider that his meanings may be interpreted long after the words have been committed to paper; moreover, he has to consider that they will be interpreted without benefit of all the nods, winks, pauses, stresses, smiles, grimaces, repetitions and rephrasings which go on all the time in speech.

4 Writing occurs in space as well as in time. It exists independently of the physical context in which it was produced and will continue to exist so long as the ink and paper, or chisel marks on stone, exist. Thus, the system has to convey meanings by means of techniques that produce permanent realizations of language, as distinct from speech, which exists only in the time it takes to produce the speech. Reproduction, from audio or videotape, is not the same event.

5 Over the centuries, the writing system of English has developed features quite unlike those present in speech. For example, when talking, we need to ease the listener's understanding by using those helpful lubrications of conversation such as 'well', 'you know', 'you see', and many more. These are not always evident in writing, however, because they are not needed so much. If one is unsure of the precise significance of a particular sentence, one can go back on the page, or over several pages, look at

preceding chapters or even different books, to help the achieving of full comprehension.

6 Writing and speech are, then, different realizations of the language system that we know as English (or whatever other language we happen to be considering) and should be regarded as being different, with as full as possible a knowledge of what those differences are. This is not the place to list the linguistic features of both systems, but if is important to remember that writing is not just a written form of speech.

7 Writing is primarily a *visual* system, as distinct from the *auditory* system of speech.

So far, we have been considering more or less theoretical characteristics of speech and writing. In real life, of course, language cannot sensibly be abstracted from the prejudices, intolerances, habits and expectations which render the study of any aspect of human behaviour so difficult. When studying language behaviour, as opposed to engaging in it, we must, however, have recourse to some form of analysis, and be aware of our own attitudes and prejudices; what is important is that we be clear about both our analytic approach and our attitudes towards the 'mess' or 'fuzz' which accompanies language activity. If we wish to discuss the teaching and learning of writing, we need to be clear about two particular issues — the use and status of standard English, and the notion of correctness.

There has been a tendency, in recent times, and for a variety of reasons, to decry the value and importance of standard English. One of the reasons is a misunderstanding of an important linguistic fact, which is that no language is *linguistically* better or worse than any other. This fact, accepted by linguists, needs to be amplified. What linguists mean by saying that all languages are equal is that each language studied is governed by sets of rules which, no matter what the status or state of social development attained by the language community using that language, are usually many and complex. Whether we are considering the language of a stone age Amazonian tribe, or one of the major European languages, we are going to need complex rules to describe the sound system, the grammar, the meaning relations of utterances, and the contexts of language use.

It is, however, absurd to suppose, as some people have supposed, that that means that in any given society all forms of language are of equal use, value and prestige. In present-day Britain, and in many other parts of the English-speaking world, there are varieties of English; the more social and regional groups there are within a community, the more varieties there are likely to be. In our society, there is one variety which has a higher prestige and a greater functional value than any other, and it is called Standard English. Now, even Standard English means rather different things according to whether we are considering America, Australasia or India, for example. In Britain, it may be more useful to refer to Standard British English (SBE), to distinguish it from Standard American English, Standard Australian English, and so on. Note that we are not referring to *accent*. There are many different ways of pronouncing any variety of English; there is a parallel in speech to SBE, which linguists call 'Received Pronunciation' (RP), though laymen may call it 'speaking without an accent', and many children in our schools will simply call it 'talking posh'. Since our concern is with writing, we shall not need to concern ourselves with debates about accent.

Some people, who have learned from their reading of popular works in linguistics that 'there is no such thing as a primitive language', or that 'all languages are equal', have mistakenly come to the conclusion that all varieties of a language are equally useful. So, one comes across attempts not only to raise the status of nonstandard varieties of English, but also to diminish the value of SBE. While the first aim may be a valid one — certainly it often springs from altruistic motives — the second is foolish. There are those who would sanction, in children's writing, nonstandard usages such as *I could of* for *I could have*, or *I done* for *I did*, *we was* for *we were*, in the belief that this is freeing children from the constraints of SBE, and somehow doing something to dismantle the power structures of our society. Conversely, there are those who equate such solecisms with a disintegration of moral standards, and become unreasonably irate. Both are wrong, since both sets of views stem from a fallacious view of correctness in language.

Correctness is a difficult term to use in relation to language, because language is always changing. In one sense, whatever is spoken is correct, in that if a group within a language community habitually uses a certain form, then that form may be said to be correct for that particular language variety, though incorrect for SBE or for another variety of the language. This applies to every level of the language system — the sound system, that of word formation, of syntax, even of whole texts larger than a single sentence. But at every level there are things which are quite simply wrong. If instead of writing *he has never told a lie* I write *Khe has shelling never a lie*, I shall be wrong (incorrect) in spelling, syntax, word order and vocabulary, and I am in need of correction. For a Londoner to write *he never told no lies* may be appropriate to his dialect, but unless he is writing dialogue this sentence must be considered inappropriate in writing, and in SBE it is incorrect. Appropriateness and correctness are near synonyms; those who would wish to substitute inappropriate for incorrect are in most cases begging the question. To suggest that SBE is inappropriate for the writing of narrative English prose is to raise an entirely different question, of a sociological rather than a linguistic nature.

Writing is much less prone to change than speech, and the reasons have much to do with the importance of standard English. Writing needs, in many instances, to constitute a permanent and relatively unambiguous record; it is frequently addressed to very large readerships, of mixed linguistic background and experience, as distinct from an individual or small group, which is usually the nature of a speech audience; it has to transcend localized and national variations of dialect in order to be readily acceptable and comprehensible to people separated by distance, custom, etc. The permanence of writing, opposed to the transitoriness of speech, involves a necessary conservatism. Written forms do change, but slowly.

A further consideration is that in most parts of the English-speaking world, and especially in their education systems, writing is a crucial determinant of academic, social and economic success. Standard English has its most evident manifestation and is at its most conservative in writing, and we do children a disservice if we do not teach them how to achieve the use of standard forms in writing, whatever nonstandard usages we may allow or encourage on the way. When we come to assess their writing during the statutory years of schooling, one of the factors to be borne in mind is how well pupils have assimilated the forms of standard English. If they are clearly not writing in SBE – if, for example, they are writing dialogue – then it will become appropriate to use other forms.

There is nothing sacrosanct about any of the conventions of standard grammar, vocabulary or orthography, and they will certainly change over the years. But these conventions do exist, and they will not change so quickly as to relieve teachers from the duty of teaching children how to use them. A 15-year-old girl, writing of how she had discussed with a friend a film on arranged marriages, included in her script the following:

I arsked her: 'Dose it not worrie you that the man to whom you will marrie might be crule to you and how can you love a man that you have never seen nor know about?' (DES 1983)

The meaning of the passage is clear enough, but it is also clear that she is not able to use the standard spelling conventions of English (*arsked*, *dose*, *worrie*, *marrie*, *crule*); nor the punctuation conventions (colon, and placing of punctuation marks); nor the standard grammatical conventions (*to whom you will marrie*, *that you have never seen nor know about*). Whether we are concerned with the use of English nonstandard features in writing, as in the example just quoted, or in, say, the interference of Jamaican creole, as in much of the pupils' work quoted by John Richmond in his very stimulating book on the teaching of writing (Richmond 1982), the hard fact remains that children who have not learned to use the standard forms of our language in their writing by the time they leave school will be unable to achieve success in educational terms, and will be at a disadvantage in a society where expectations of conformity are not matched by those children's performance.

These comments on standard English and correctness should not lead the reader to suppose that what is being advocated is a censorious concentration by teachers on *eradicating* nonstandard usages, or an attempt to substitute, in any permanent way, one pattern of linguistic behaviour for another. The issue of standard English is only part of the story, and merits attention largely because crude and aggressive postures are adopted by both 'progressive' and 'reactionary' writers on language in education. My view, which is by now, I hope, clearly enough stated, is that both sets of opinions are inaccurate, and unhelpful to children. The emphasis should all the time be on extending a repertoire of language styles and usages, not on insisting on one kind of conformity or another. The important issue for teachers is how to go about extending those language repertoires. Many strategies should be adopted — from taking delight, with young children, in language differences, by looking at different ways of 'saying the same thing', or considering rhymes, jingles, proverbs (many of which are of dialectal origin), to a conscious and enjoyable consideration, with older pupils, of how usages vary from region to region, and from individual to individual. Responding to written forms has a part to play here. Instead of putting a red line through an inappropriate dialectal usage, some pointers to social, situational and linguistic contexts might be given; looking at contrasting, but effective usages from published texts might help; deliberately *inappropriate* forms might enjoyably be examined. It does not really matter what tactics are used, so long as the emphasis is on extending and not restricting pupils' linguistic experience and competence.

3
Functions of language

Most teachers would probably agree with the notion advanced in the introductory chapter that teaching involves assessment of some kind. Not all of them, however, would think of assessment as being rooted in the process of teaching, rather than as a single event (say, marking an essay), or as a set of events (say, arriving at an examination grade on the basis of a set of marked papers). Assessment, in the sense in which it is being used in this book, means more than marking essays. It may involve that, of course, but it may also involve making a decision during a lesson on why a specific pupil has written a particular word in a particular way; it may involve forming some idea of what a pupil needs (and that need may be different from the needs of the rest of the class) in the way of practice over the following two or three weeks. It is, in other words, an inescapable aspect of classroom practice. For that reason, if for no other, it is not possible to provide an exhaustive list of instructions, a ready-to-use inventory of items for the instant recording of achievement.

Another reason why it is not possible to give a complete and ready system is concerned with the nature of language use. Language, whether spoken or written, occurs meaningfully in real life when communication of some kind is needed or is desired. The communication may be with other people, as it usually is, or with oneself; sometimes the message itself is more important than the expression of it, as in a request for information, and at other times — usually in speech — what is said is less important than the speaker's wish to please, impress, insult, etc. There is an indefinitely large number of purposes for which language is used; so while we can categorize the purely formal *linguistic* features of what is said or written, we cannot do the same in relation to the *functions* which language serves. Nonetheless, for teaching purposes it is necessary to have some sort of categorization of writing functions, for a number of reasons. Learning how to write well is dependent upon actually doing it when you need or wish to do it. As Geoffrey Thornton states (1980, 29):

> One learns to write by writing. It is only by trying to write in response to need that one can explore for oneself the two constraints, namely, what the writing system will allow, and what our own mastery of the writing system will allow us to do.

Now if, during school years, pupils are to practise writing, then there has to be a variety of contexts. One cannot usefully say to anyone 'Write!', without specifying a situation in which and a topic upon which to write. Writing has to be about something. Moreover, it is not enough to provide contexts for writing if what is produced is going to be the same kind of writing all the time. A good football player has to practise in order to acquire accuracy when kicking a ball; but he also has to practise doing different things in order to achieve adequate levels of performance when running, heading a ball, tackling an opposing player, evading a tackle, altering pace, feinting, and so on. The player who spends all his time practising for accuracy when kicking a ball, and nothing else. will not be much good during a real football match. There has to be variety in training, not just for football players, but for children who are learning to write. This means writing for different purposes, and, since time is limited − after all, a pupil is in the classroom for only 25−30 hours in a week, and for much of that time doing things other than writing − it is up to the teacher to select. But on what basis should selection be made?

It is an important question, since assessment is not just a matter of seeing how well pupils can use commas and full stops; it is, more importantly, a question of seeing how appropriately, how flexibly, how discriminatingly, how accurately, and how confidently they can use the resources of the writing system for desired and defined purposes. In other words, assessment is rooted in the *process* of teaching, as well as being an evaluation of the writing *product*. So, on what basis does one provide contexts for writing? The answer will, to an extent, determine the kind of assessment used; what assessment is used will also be determined by a number of other factors, such as one's notion of the purposes of language, one's concern with the features of linguistic form, and matters of organization and classroom procedure. In deciding how well a piece of writing is doing its job, we take different issues simultaneously into account, and for the most part without giving very much thought to what those issues are or how they interrelate. When the Assessment of Performance Unit's results and techniques were commented on in the Department of Education and Science publication 'How well can 15-year-olds write?' (DES 1983), a letter written as to a prospective employer, asking for a summer job was included.

16th November 1981

Dear Sir

    I am applying for ~~the~~ your summer job of ~~Com~~ the Manchester and South Yorkshire Chamber of Commerce and Industry the position that intrests me is the ~~construction work~~ engineering part I am suitable for this post because I am stud~~ing~~ing commerce at school. I am available most weeks days except fridays. I ~~am~~ has also very good at Technical Drawing and I hope to pass an O' level in that subject. well I hope to hear from your firm soon to say if I hae got the job or not So untill then I will say ~~cheers~~ goodbye hope to be hearing from you soon yours faithfully

There are, among the many things to be said about this letter, three features which stand out. First, there is the cheerful but quite inappropriate style — inappropriate, that is, to the purpose of the letter, which is to persuade someone to give the writer a job. Second, and closely related to the first, is the apparent failure to contextualize the task, i.e. to take into account the ages, social functions and occupational requirements of addressor and addressee. At least, the writer may have had in mind the potential employer, but has, for whatever reasons, displayed no knowledge of the needs of the situation. Third, there are the purely formal (i.e. relating to form) linguistic aspects of the text — the layout, the spelling, the sentence-structure, the choice of words, and so forth. When reading a piece of prose, we do not normally consider such aspects separately; but if it is our job to help writers such as this one to write more effectively, then for practical purposes we have to take things one a time at the 'pre-operational' stage, that is, when we are preparing, planning, reflecting.

Statistics from the Assessment of Performance Unit show that children nationally score far more highly on knowledge of grammatical conventions than on their ability to display appropriateness of style. Since this is so, it seems to be a matter of common sense that we should be paying much more attention than is usually paid in schools to developing pupils' abilities to achieve a flexibility of written style that will enable them to write appropriately for a variety of purposes.

What purposes? There have been many attempts to devise sound theoretical models of language functions. Michael Halliday, in an earlier volume in this series (Halliday 1973) lists seven 'models of language' built up and needed by children. They are:

1 The instrumental — in which language is conceived of as a means of getting things done, what Halliday calls the 'I want' function.
2 The regulatory — by which language is used as a means of controlling behaviour, the 'do as I tell you' function.
3 The interactional — this self-explanatory term is characterized as the 'me and you' function.
4 The personal — this is closely related to the interactional model, and is the expression of the writer's individual personality, what Halliday calls the 'here I come' function.
5 The heuristic — the heuristic use of language is that which enables one to learn, to obtain a firmer grasp on the world, what is termed the 'tell me why' function.
6 The imaginative — a use of language which also relates to the child's increasing experience of the world, but in a different way, a way in which he restructures experience through language. We can call this the 'let's pretend' function.
7 The representational — by this, Halliday refers to what is perhaps the commonest adult model of language. Indeed, for some it is the only one. It relates to language which communicates content, which expresses propositions, which conveys messages — the 'I've got something to tell you' function.

It is as well to digress a little here in order to comment on some terms which have already been frequently used in this chapter — viz. 'model', 'function' and 'use' (or 'purpose'). The word 'model' has been used to refer to some simplified image of language, acquired by a knowledge of what language does. The term has a specific technical sense in scientific and linguistic theory, but that need not concern us here. 'Function' is a fashionable word, and is also ambiguous. Although in mathematics and in linguistics the term has for many years been used in a clear and specific sense, it has come into prominence in educational writings on language in the last couple of decades as a way of referring to what language *does* as distinct from what it *is*. In this later sense, it accords with the informal, everyday use of the word, as when we ask, 'What is her function in the school?', or, 'What is the function of this committee?'. When applied to language itself it has a different sense, referring to abstract relationships among grammatical elements. Those readers who are familiar with Halliday's work will know that he points out (1973) that for the adult language — he is writing in the book mainly about the earlier stages of language development — the notion of function has to be refined, and can no longer be equated with use, but has to be used as a more abstract concept. However, for our purposes it will do no harm to use, henceforth, the terms 'function', 'use' and 'purpose' interchangeably, since all three will be used in their everyday senses.

Much of what Halliday has to say is valuable to teachers, and is always interesting. The scheme referred to above has not however really passed into common classroom currency.

Another functional model of language mentioned earlier (see chapter 1, p. 17) is that associated with James Britton. In his framework, the terms 'expressive', 'transactional' and 'poetic' are used to refer to the ways in which children use language; at first, claims Britton, children use language as a manifestation of their own personalities (the expressive function) and then in more impersonal, 'public' ways (transactional). When they learn to structure language in a way which throws into prominence the 'shaped' or deliberated *form* of what is being written, whether by means of a story, a poem or an essay, they are said to be using language in its poetic function. Whatever the merits and demerits of the model, it should be noted that in secondary schools the thinking of many English departments has been affected by it. Primary teachers may be more familiar with the work of Joan Tough, whose categorization of language uses has found favour with many schools (see Tough 1977).

The fact is that it is not possible to make an exhaustive and definitive categorization of uses of language. Consider a period of time during an ordinary day in your own life. You may be surprised how, in the course of an hour or two, depending on your occupation, the people you talk to, and your own needs and wishes, the uses to which you put your linguistic resources increases in number. From leaving the house in the morning you may within the space of a couple of hours do the following: greet people, request information, give directions, ask for directions, request a service, inform people, persuade, argue, cajole, insult, apologise, narrate, threaten, demand, exclaim, joke, talk to yourself, or even use silence purposefully. The above list represents my informal categorization of a friend's use of language, over the space of a couple of hours. No doubt the list would have lengthened throughout the day.

We must have some sort of inventory of uses, however, if we are to help pupils to extend their range of language use, assuming that it is agreed that this is one of the chief duties of any teacher. It is easier to do this for writing than it is for speech. For one thing, speech is usually an interactive process, a face-to-face exchange of words in which each speaker modifies his or her language rapidly according to how the listener's reactions are being perceived. When writing, we are communicating at a distance in both space and time. We have the time to alter a phrase here, add a word there, delete a sentence somewhere else. We usually know to whom we are writing, though the precision of that knowledge varies, of course. In the case of a letter to an individual, we know exactly, unless it is to someone we have never met, while when writing a book or an article, we are addressing ourselves to whoever can be persuaded to buy it. Writing is more amenable to analysis of whatever kind, and it is much easier to categorize writing uses than to attempt to do the same for talking and listening.

It is worth considering an already existing instrument of categorization and assessment possessed by teachers, which is their own informed experience. Paradoxically, that valuable resource militates against the construction of an agreed inventory of language uses. The main reason for this is that there comes a point, in almost every discussion of educational matters, at which philosophical and social beliefs and attitudes are seen to be determining the course of an argument. They do so all the time, of course, but it usually takes a while for them to become apparent. The framing of a curriculum, for example, depends upon what we take to be the purposes of education. Are schools to reflect accepted social values, or to change them? In any case, *whose* accepted values, since we all have a different notion of what constitutes 'our society'?

Decisions on such questions have to be decided by whom? So the questions multiply, and so it is with language.

Very often, statements made about the functions of language derive from assumptions or beliefs that seem to have little to do with either language or education. They stem from views of what society is thought to be, or what someone would like society to be. Such views frequently determine the bases or premises of linguistic decisions. This means that there is a high degree of subjectivity informing most accounts of language use applicable to the classroom.

There is, then, no point in trying to devise a framework of assessment which is wholly objective, since what has been said about education in general, and language in particular, applies to the process of assessment just as well. One could of course secure agreement, on wholly objective grounds, to aspects of writing which are trivial or very detailed.

For example, it would be possible to construct a checklist of items referring to such things as the length of paragraphs, or the extent to which pupils produce mis-spellings of a given corpus of words. But it would not be worth doing.

Moreover, attempts to devise a procedure for assessing any aspect of natural language other than the trivial, in either speech or writing, are grounded, if they seek wholly to eliminate subjectivity, on a misunderstanding of the nature of real-life language use. Although more readily apparent in respect of the spoken language, it is true of all language that it is realized in a context of situation by people whose responses (including teachers responding to pupils' writing) have been modified and moulded by all of their previous experience. The native speaker acquires stereotypical linguistic expectations over a lifetime.

It is worth noting how the word 'stereotype' has gathered unfavourable connotations in recent times. In one way that is unfortunate, since the notion of stereotype is very important. It is useful to recall the primary, historical sense of the word, originating in the printing industry. When the solid metal plates were cast from the papier-mâché moulds, so that large numbers of copies could be run off, the plates themselves were called the stereotypes (from the Greek *stereos*, meaning 'solid'). Now, there is a process analogous to that in language. When we have learned to read, we begin to fashion a mould of expectations, as we keep on encountering, day after day, and year after year, different language forms used in different contexts, for different purposes. That is, we generalize, from our countless reading/writing experiences, as we form patterns in our minds. Life would be impossible otherwise.

So it is with teachers. Over the years, they too have built up expectations of good writers and poor writers, of different ages and in different contexts. It is too often assumed that subjective judgements are suspect, as if subjectivity were a kind of shameful vice, and in any case not to be admitted to when dealing with the business of assessment. But judgements are, by definition, subjective. They are inadequate if the experience, knowledge and insights informing them are inadequate. But a teacher whose intuitions are informed by knowledge of the pupils being taught, whose expertise is sufficient for the purpose, and who has some principles for guidance, possesses a powerful instrument of assessment in those intuitions.

Difficulties still remain, however. Not all teachers have the necessary informing experience to render their judgements valid. Perhaps a way of approaching the issues of how we categorize writing purposes would be to look at them from the point of view of what in practice is actually demanded of pupils in schools. Such a 'task-orientated' approach has the advantage of being immediately close to the professional concerns of teachers. This is all right if we can agree that what teachers do is what they *should* be doing. But this is not always the case. In the report which was published following the national survey of aspects of secondary school work by H M Inspectorate (DES 1979) we find that:

> The common pattern of instruction restricts the pupil's opportunities of experiencing and even more of using the language he needs. (p. 83)

This was said in reference to writing; in amplifying this comment, the report went on to list the total written output of an able 15-year-old boy in the second term of his fourth year:

> 3.9 This pattern of instruction may be illustrated by an example of the writing of an able boy in the second term of his fourth year. It is an example which could too easily be replicated, with only slight variations.

> *English*
> Written output of about 6000 words, but including seven punctuation, thirteen comprehension, two grammar and three

multiple choice exercises calling for little of the pupil's own writing.

History
Notes and essays − about 10,000 words.

French
Some 6000 words − mainly in short sentences and occasional paragraphs.

Geography
A book of 2300 words of copied statements.

Physics
A file of notes (all of which were copied) and problems adding up to 3000 words: a brief file describing five experiments coming to 500 words.

Music
A book of 10,000 words of copied notes, some (with the teacher's approval) copied from the book of another pupil who had taken the course the year before.

Mathematics
Three exercise books, although naturally enough with far less text.

The chief criticism among several implied by the above quotation is that the range of writing tasks is too narrow. The quantity is enormous, but half of it was dictated and the rest falls within a very narrow range of language use. Things have changed little in the years since that pupil penned his 36,000 words; the work-sampling procedures of the Assessment of Performance Unit are yielding the same pattern. This makes it necessary to repeat that different writing purposes call for different exploitation of the features of linguistic form, which can be mastered by apprentice writers only if the use of those features is practised in meaningful contexts. To be sure that our pupils get the necessary practice, we need to ensure that they write for a wide range of purposes. To avoid aimlessness or randomness in this area, some guiding principles are necessary.

It is suggested that on the way to developing a mode of assessment, we should have in mind four general concerns: first, the curricular needs of and demands made upon pupils, as far as writing is concerned; second, adult expectations in respect of writing; third, the implications of the ways in which those expectations are realized; and fourth, the linguistic features which relate to those realizations. Before moving, in this chapter, to a simple framework of writing purposes, let us briefly consider those four points.

1 Curricular needs

In thinking of the written language in relation to curricular needs and requirements, we are taken back to the Bullock Report of 1975 (DES 1975), in which chapter 12 is entitled 'Language across the curriculum'. In that chapter, the final paragraph contained the recommendation that 'a policy for language across the curriculum should be adopted by every school' (p. 193). Unfortunately, many initiatives which followed were based on false assumptions. It was assumed by many teachers and some local authorities that the production of a document constituted the development of a policy. It is an apparently widespread fallacy to assume that producing a document necessarily entails action. It was also widely thought that subject departments in secondary schools should somehow contribute towards the language development of pupils. In fact, the converse of that notion was what was really being suggested – that the important question was not, 'How can geographers, physicists, home economists, etc. contribute to language development?' but rather, 'How can a consideration of the relationship between the learning of geography, physics, home economics, etc. and the language demands made by those subjects help pupils to learn better?'

In an attempt to find out more about the language needs and experience of pupils, several techniques were used. Some of the results were very revealing. Following a pupil through a complete school day, going to every class and activity, shows us that the bulk of time is spent by children listening to teachers talking; it also shows that the writing demands are narrow. If one collects the total written output of a pupil in a secondary school over, say, half a term, one can see that most of the writing falls into three main categories, which we can informally characterize as *(i)* recording facts, *(ii)* factual narrative, *(iii)* summarizing information derived either from exercises or from teachers. In the case of primary-age pupils, there is likely to be a more frequent incidence of story-writing; but even so, one is struck by the narrowness of the larger proportion of writing tasks demanded of children, from the age of 9 to 16. Obviously, a great deal depends on the curricular philosophy of the school, and even more on individual teachers' methods. Allowing for the enormous variety of approach which is possible within the British system, one can urge that there is a general need to extend the range of writing tasks so that pupils can more flexibly and competently meet the writing demands of their curricula.

2 Expectations

We have already mentioned the subjective nature of usual teacher assessment. Yet, with all the variations inherent in any subjective evaluation, most teachers would probably agree, to a surprisingly large extent, on what constitutes good or bad writing.

There are, of course some norms so generally agreed that no problems arise. It would be hard to find a school in which, when pupils are being taught the conventions of letter-writing, teachers do not tell them that a letter beginning 'Dear Sir' or 'Dear Madam' always ends with 'Your faithfully'. Other areas of usage are less certain, for example the extent to which colloquialisms are admissible in different contexts, or more generally, what degrees of formality and informality are desirable in different contexts. It is important that in working towards a framework of assessment we consider how far pupils are being prepared to meet the expectations with regard to writing of further and higher education, of employers, of all the agencies with which a socially competent person will have to deal in the world as it is (rather than the world as we might like it to be).

3 Realizing expectations

It was claimed earlier that language varies according to *why* it is used and to *who* is using it. If we take only one use of writing, such as communication of information, it is clear that the mode of expression will vary according to the social context not only of the 'communication event' but also of the person communicating. If we think of an event such as a parent writing to a teacher, asking for information about some aspect of a child's work, the language used will to some extent be affected by the age, sex, social class and occupation of the writer. A teacher, computer analyst, shopkeeper, antique dealer, policeman, estate agent, doctor will each use language in different ways. *What* is being written about will certainly affect choices made in the writing. The businessman writing about his daughter's homework is hardly likely to use phrases such as 'cost benefit analysis' or 'production fall-off in the last quarter of the year'. If he does use such instances of occupational vocabulary — or jargon — he is guilty of not paying attention to a crucial element in successful written expression, consideration of one's readership. For every piece of writing we should consider *who*, *what*, and *for whom*. Who, because we are all products of our own experience, and that experience may have constrained our writing style; what, because each piece of writing is setting out to fulfill some aim, however trivial or important; for whom, because in all human transactions, including language transactions, we are more likely to fulfill our aims if we enter into the situational context of the other person, or group, or, in the case of writing, readership. In fact we do, of course, take these factors into account in real life, but we do so unconsciously. When teaching others to write effectively, those factors have to be made explicit. Much of what happens in the classroom is necessarily artificial, and may seem to have little to do with 'real life'. The more that a task approximates to what pupils consider to be realistic activity, the more successful is likely to be the writing. So that, if a story written in school is going to be read by, and preferably to, another group of pupils, or visitors to the school, or is to be included in a magazine, it is likely that the writer's attention will be more sharply focussed on the appropriateness of vocabulary, grammar, layout, etc.

4 Linguistic features

All writing involves choice, at different levels. The fifth-year examination candidate who wrote:

> The Macbeths had had the Duncans round for drinks that night, and everyone was feeling pretty high. . . .

has made not a single error in spelling, punctuation or grammar. The choices of language made, however, have resulted in language which, though entirely appropriate for the recounting of events at a successful cocktail party the previous week, is not appropriate to a literary account of Duncan's murder in Shakespeare's tragedy. The errors may occur at several levels of language, sometimes at a relatively low level of complexity. The 12-year-old who wrote:

> That night, I was walking down the road quiet peacefully, when suddenly from behind the the trees the dreaded monster lept out upon me

shows a command of grammatical usage that is perfectly acceptable. The subordinate clause, the placing of adverbial phrases, and the overall structure of the sentence are all correct. Apart from the repetition of *the*, presumably due more to carelessness than ignorance, his only errors are in the choice and order of letters within words, i.e. in spelling.

We shall address specifically linguistic topics in the next chapter. It is enough at this point to note that there are two general aspects of writing that we have been considering. First, those 'external to the text' — such matters as consideration of readership or importance of context — and those 'internal to the text', in which, regardless of the topic, the readership, the attitudes, views, and origins of the writer, there are some features which can be correct or incorrect according to the conventions of our writing system.

One such feature is spelling. While it is certainly true that much time is wasted through the use of inadequate methods to teach pupils to spell correctly (uncontextualized words to be 'learned', writing out a word three times, etc.) there is no doubt that pupils, if they are to be said to have mastered the writing system, need to learn how to spell. What is usually at issue is not whether but how we teach them (see Thornton 1980, chapter 6). Another 'internal' feature relates to such grammatical phenomena as verb tense, the structure of noun phrases and the use of adverbial expressions. When we consider the main difficulties experienced by pupils, most of those difficulties lie in making successful links between the outside world and the language choices made. So the examination candidate who wrote accurately, though inappropriately, about Macbeth has made a faulty link between the language to be used and adult expectations of the genre of literary criticism. However, consider the statement

> He writes every week

The choice of *he* in that statement relates to the world outside. It is *he* because the word refers to a male person existing in the world. But *writes* is different. It is *writes* and not *write* because in standard English there is agreement between a 3rd person subject, *he*, and the present tense verb form, realized by the letter *s* added to the verb stem. The fact that we mark a verb with a final -*s* when there is a 3rd person singular subject has nothing to do with the outside world and everything to do with the internal patterns of English syntax. The 12-year-old writing about the monster was making errors concerned with the 'internal' aspect of language organization, though not, in his case, at the level of syntax.

In the light of those four areas of concern, which have sufficient importance for them to serve as guiding principles, we can now move to an informal categorization of language uses. But before commenting on the categories to be suggested, one further point needs to be made. In any assessment activity, we have to bear in mind that pupils are developing their powers of thought and language, and that they differ in their individual rates of progress. Developmental factors are important in any educational process, though we should also remember that individual children may not, indeed will not conform to the statistical averages of developmental psychologists. In what follows, however, some attention has been paid, as will be seen from the ordering of the categories, to developmental features of children's language activity.

For the purposes of arriving at an assessment framework, then, our range of writing purposes may be broadly categorized under six headings.

(i) Recording. By this is meant any factual relaying of events. The seven-year-old who laboriously prints, *Last night I watched TV* is recording. So is the sixth-form physics student who writes, *The plane wave . . . appeared to diverge from a point behind the surface F, which is the principal focus of the convex surface.* In the second clause of that statement, the writer is also describing, of course. Indeed, the more complex the writing, the more the writing will fall into more than one category. But there will be a predominant category.

(ii) Instructional. This term is used, as are the others, in its everyday sense. Giving instructions in writing ranges from: *To get to the post office, you turn right at the lights and take the second road on the left* to technical manuals of staggering complexity. In any literate society, the use of written instruction is important. In schools it is often vital, though the understanding of written instructions is probably more vital than the ability to write them.

However, under this category may be included not merely instructions, in the sense of commands, but also the relaying to another person or group of persons of all manner of factual information. For some adults, the transmission of factual information may well be the only written use of language. So we may call this category the 'instructional/transmissional', which, in the computer age now falling upon us, could be mnemonically abbreviated to I/T.

(iii) Narrative/descriptive. Most description occurs as part of writing which can be characterized as narrative prose. Of course, recording may take the form of narration, as in some diaries; description may be undertaken without any narrative. But bear in mind that we are discussing this in the context of assessing writing in schools, where pupils are rarely completely autonomous authors, but usually writing to meet the needs of a teacher-assigned task. It is better if tasks are mutually agreed; this does not mean that children should write whatever drifts into their heads, but that better writing emerges from a mutually negotiated understanding of what is required. Description may be purely factual, at a rudimentary level, or may, in content and form, be fulfilling a literary purpose. For some older pupils the latter may apply, but it is still worth having a separate category for the kind of prose which sets out to narrate, descriptively or not, a sequence of events.

(iv) Explanatory/argument. It is of considerable importance that opportunities are provided in school to write explanations (preferably for a known readership). The writing of explanatory prose enables children to clarify their own thoughts, to come to conclusions, in short to make use of a learning tool. The result will be an ability not only to provide understandable accounts and explanations of events and processes, but also, at the most advanced level, to produce coherent and reasoned argument. If the contexts in which such writing takes place are realistic enough, it may clarify aspects of experience for the reader. It will also enable the writer to express views on the basis of rational consideration rather than *ad hoc* reaction. Argument, in this sense, does not of course mean polemic, but rather a logically valid series of propositions and deductions. Argument may become polemical, or draw on feelings rather than reason, especially if a motive underlying the writing is persuasion.

(v) Persuasive. As pupils grow older and more certain of their capacity to use their linguistic resources, the more linguistic power they can wield. The more, also, can they perceive the linguistic designs which others may have upon them — advertisers, sales-

men, politicians, even teachers! Just as they should be helped to recognize the force of valid argument and the defects of spurious argument, so they ought to be helped to develop the techniques of persuasive writing for themselves, in order to marshal good reasons for supporting their own beliefs, behaviour or proposals.

(vi) Literary/imaginative. For some pupils, it may be possible to use written language in such a way that its *form*, in either prose or verse, is so inextricably and smoothly linked to content that the writing becomes both memorable and capable of reflecting, even recreating some aspect of experience. Poets, novelists and playwrights are people who are able to do this. All pupils in schools can *try* to do it, however modest or unsuccessful in adult literary terms the results may be, and it is important that they do try, for at least four reasons: first, it helps them to achieve a flexibility of language that is transferable to other language uses; second, it can enable them to enlarge and understand their own responses to experience; third, it can help them to read literature more critically; fourth, it can give enormous pleasure, which is not only to be valued for itself, but can powerfully increase motivation. This applies to the ten-line fairy story written in the infant or junior classroom as much as it does to the most sophisticated product of the sixth-form English Literature class.

At this point, someone may be exclaiming, 'But what about making notes, what about writing business letters, what about a dozen other writing tasks that I could mention?' The fact is that we have to be concerned for assessment purposes with *types* of language use. The tasks mentioned by the objecting reader can be subsumed under one (or more than one) of the six types discussed above. Given these six types of writing purposes, it is possible to cover a range of writing activities wide enough for the purpose of assment in school. They are sufficiently general to cover most, if not all, of the writing activities associated with both primary and secondary curricula. The important thing is that the choice is not random, as I hope the foregoing discussion of classroom demands and curricular needs will have illustrated. Much depends on underlying educational principles. If one believes that a subject-based view of the curriculum is more important than anything else, then the categories may emerge as 'historical prose' or 'technical description' or 'scientific reporting'. If one believes that notions of personal growth and development are more important than anything else, a different set will emerge. It depends on your starting point. The advantage of the six categories proposed is that they can encompass all the others in the light of the principles mentioned earlier.

In real life, we do not proceed from a set of categories to a set of activities or patterns of behaviour. The activities and the behaviour occur and the categories come later from those who wish to reflect upon, or explain, or assess the behaviour. So it is most important that we do not confuse the order of any theoretical presentation with real-life ordering of events. It is necessary for teachers to map onto pupils' behaviour some sort of categorization, otherwise we shall simply react, in haphazard and inconsistent ways. Furthermore, the six categories (indeed any categories) are neither sequential nor exclusive. This is worth restating. One should not think that the pupil will move, say, from simple recording to narrative to argument. But any writing task may well be *predominantly* instructional or *predominantly* persuasive, so that in the course of a term, or a year, a teacher may be able legitimately to say that x number of narrative pieces and y number of persuasive pieces have been written by pupil A, or group B.

The next chapter will focus on the linguistic features, as distinct from the functional features of writing. After a consideration of the linguistic areas of concern, we shall be in a position to suggest a framework for writing assessment.

Summary

1a Various attempts have been made to devise models of language functions (cf. Halliday, Britton *et al.*).

1b It is not possible to make an exhaustive and definitive list or categorization of language function, but *some* categorization is essential.

2a There is no point in attempting a wholly objective framework of assessment, since much depends on beliefs and assumptions which are prior to any linguistic or pedagogical point of view.

2b Importance should be attached to teachers' own *informed intuitions*.

3a There needs to be a wide range of writing activities and purposes in the classroom.

3b We need some principles for guidance, viz.

    (i)   curricular needs and demands
    (ii) helping pupils to approximate to adult expectations
    (iii) need to contextualize writing activities

(iv)   need to consider linguistic form in relation to those activities.

3c Developmental factors need to be borne in mind.

4a We can categorize writing functions as *(i)* recording, *(ii)* instructional, *(iii)* narrative descriptive, *(iv)* explanatory argument, *(v)* persuasive, *(vi)* literary/imaginative.

4b The categories are neither exclusive nor sequential.

4
Some linguistic features of writing

We have been discussing writing as it refers to human experience, to the world outside, as it were. Certainly, if a person is to be effective in the written mode of language, he needs to be able to write for a variety of purposes, as discussed in the previous chapter. But now we must look at the world inside the text, the language used. Let us consider a piece of writing composed by a second-year pupil in a London secondary school.

It all started when we were all walking down a back street. That is me, Angela, Angele, Donna and Joanne. We was all coming from a party. These boys were comming up behind us so we started to run where we come up the main road. Joanne said "come on. Let's go and get some food from the chip shop. So we all went in to the shop and ordered chiken and chips five times.

This constitutes rather less than a quarter of the whole piece, which was written as a story. There is no doubt that the extract quoted recounts, without much or indeed any hindrance to understanding, a series of events. Much of it is free from error; but errors there are, and it may be illuminating to look at them in some detail. If we were to seek out every error in these lines, we might compile a list such as the following

1. Spelling errors:	l. 3 *comming* for *coming*
	l. 6 *chiken* for *chicken*
2. Punctuation errors:	l. 4 *'come. . . . for' Come . . .*
	l. 4 *Lets* for *let's*
	l. 5 omission of inverted commas after *chip shop*

3. Grammatical errors: l. 2 *we was* for *we were*
                       l. 3 *These boys* for *Some boys*

One might also wish to comment on the structure of the first two sentences and the ambiguity of the third clause in the third sentence − *where we come up the main road.*

Some people may wish to call into question other aspects of the text, and others may not regard some of the errors listed as errors at all. For example, it is entirely likely that *we was coming* faithfully reflects a dialectal feature of the pupil's usual language. We shall return to that later. For the moment it is clear that *(a)* there are some errors and *(b)* the errors are not all of the same kind.

Spelling and punctuation

If we consider both the spelling and the punctuation, we see that writing *comming* for *coming* in no way affects the meaning or the clarity of the text. Similarly, the lower case *c* at the beginning of the direct speech in l. 4, and the omission of the apostrophe in *Lets* provide no obstacle to immediate understanding. It is simply that there is a lack of conformity with the conventions of English orthography. That lack, however, is an important one. It is important not because any great linguistic violence is done, nor because communication is impeded, nor yet because there exists a set of logical, unbreakable rules. What we should consider is the powerful effect of adult expectation. In the minds of most people there is an accumulation of folklore about language and very many people equate deviant spelling with ignorance, or lack of intelligence. The correspondence columns of many newspapers frequently contain expressions of outrage at 'declining standards in spelling' and equate the purported decline with lowering of educational standards in general. One instance of mis-spelling which is a potent source of adult wrath is *could of* for *could have*, as in

If you had arrived yesterday, we could of gone swimming.

This is a case of pronunciation affecting spelling. In English, most unstressed vowel sounds approximate to the sound linguists call 'schwa', (written phonetically as [ə]) which we find in the second syllable of *father* or *mother*, or in *of* in *a cup of tea*. Very few people pronounce that particular *of* as anything but [əv] ('a cup'v tea'). We do the same with *have* when this word is used before a verb to mark a past tense — 'we could've gone swimming'.

In none of these instances of mis-spelling is communication impeded. But it is as well to be clear about the educational significance of misspelling. Correct spelling is held to be important by many adults who may make decisions affecting pupils' futures. The fact that before the eighteenth century we did not have a standardized spelling system is neither here nor there. There has arisen over the past two hundred years a very strong social convention with regard to the use of standardized spellings, and learning that convention (see Stubbs 1980, 68−9) is part of becoming a literate person.

Much the same applies to punctuation. English marks off direct speech by means of 'speech marks' or inverted commas — '. . .'. Other languages use different conventions, such as ≪ . . . ≫ or by a fresh, indented line for each utterance. Obviously, there is no moral ascendancy attached to inverted commas, and the other associated conventions of writing 'direct speech', but again the fact is that that is what is expected by teachers, examiners, parents, employers and others, and we do children a disservice if we do not teach them the conventions. In punctuation, as in spelling, some of our conventional signs are more important than others. The use of the comma, for example, may be a crucial factor in conveying an accurate meaning.

The pupils in this class who omitted a comma will be punished may mean that two or three unfortunates will be chastised. But if we see *The pupils in this class, who omitted a comma, will be punished*, then a whole class of pupils is due for retribution. The comma remains a convention, in that we could all decide that henceforth wherever we used to use commas we shall now all insert small triangles. In that case, the use of the 'punctuating triangle' would have to be taught in exactly the same way as we now teach the use of the comma. It doesn't matter what the sign is, so long as its function is understood and consistently applied.

Grammar

In the quotation at the beginning of this chapter the pupil has written, in 2.2, *we was coming*. As was mentioned earlier, the use of *was* instead of the standard *were* for the 1st person plural is a feature of many dialects. Probably more people use '*was*' than '*were*'. Is it, therefore, grammatically wrong? Well, yes and no. It is not wrong in the pupil's own dialect. But it is inappropriate in this context. Referring back to what was said earlier in chapter 3, about the importance of matching style to purpose, which involves knowing what the readership is to be, it is clear that the introduction of dialectal features into a narrative story is, unless for purposes of establishing a character, not appropriate. To take another example, it is a feature of London dialect that, while in a standard form one would expect to find either an article, or a general determiner such as *some*, one finds *this* or *these*, as, for example, in:

> There's this shop in Oxford Street where you can get these really cheap jeans.

In the standard form, one would read:

> There's a shop in Oxford Street where you can get (*some*) really cheap jeans.

So, while dialectally acceptable, *we was coming* is, in a standard English narrative, similarly inappropriate. If, however, we come across the statement:

> There's a shop in Oxford Street where you can get some cheap really jeans

then we could legitimately call it wrong. The word order of English requires that we place *really* before *cheap* and not after it. It is grammatically *wrong* to produce the phrase *cheap really jeans*. In this case, it is not a sociolinguistic matter of dialect form as distinct from standard form, but of correct as distinct from incorrect.

It is self-evident that grammatical structure will vary according to the kinds of sentences used in writing on a specified topic in relation to a given purpose. As to how we specify the particular grammatical features to look for, there is clearly no way of doing that short of producing a full descriptive grammar of the English language. What we need are some guiding principles which will allow us to make consistent decisions about how well a pupil is able to observe the grammatical conventions and rules of written English.

Such principles are available from consistent descriptions of the structure of the language as expressed by descriptive linguists. Readers are referred to Quirk *et al.* (1972) for the most comprehensive available descriptive grammar of English. With our own experience of competent writing, from all sources, we see that in relation to the language system competent writers consistently do three things:

(i)   They observe patterns of word order and word structure.
(ii) They indicate without ambiguity the relations between elements of sentences (words, phrases, clauses etc.), i.e. they have a command of sentence structure.
(iii) They preserve a coherence both within and between sentences so that a text carries meaning.

Lack of space precludes more than one or two illustrative examples of each, but comments on these three points may be useful.

(i) Word order. The native English speaker's sense of what is right or not is very rarely inadequate. When confronted by a phrase such as *those four brick ugly buildings*, it is not difficult for most people to adjust the adjectives to the more normal *those four ugly brick buildings*. If asked why the second version *is* more normal than the first, most people would, I suppose, say, 'Well, it sounds better.' That is true; but the reason for its sounding better is that it is more normal, so that does not really get us very far. And in any case it is as well for teachers to have as explicit as possible a knowledge of everything to do with their own language. The reason why the second sounds better than the first is that there are four kinds of adjective which can precede a noun, or four 'slots' if you like, which can be filled. Obviously they do not have to be filled, but if any of them are, it will be in the following order:

(a)   qualifying or specifying words such as *the*, *this*, *a*, *some*, *my*, *her*. Such words are often called determiners.
(b)   the numeral type of adjective: *two*, *ten*, *fifth* etc.
(c)   the ordinary describing epithets, such as *pretty*, *difficult*, *cracked*. Most of the thousands of English words which can be labelled as adjectives fall into this category.
(d)   those which in another phrase could stand, unaltered, as nouns, e.g. *brick*, *stone*, *family*.

All adjectives which occur before a noun fall into one of the above four categories, and *always in that order*. Any noun phrase will fit the framework:

a (determiners) $+$ b (numeral) $+$ c (epithet) $+$ d (nominal) $+$ N(noun)

a	b	c	d	N
my	—	best	—	coat
those	two	—	family	saloons
those	four	ugly	brick	buildings

As far as word structure is concerned, faulty grasp of structure frequently mainfests itself through misspellings, when, for example, pupils write words such as *nationel* (for *national*). Stubbs 1980 (following Keen 1978, 42ff.) shows how pupils might be helped by displays of sets of related words. If someone writes *medesin* (for *medicine*), we could start with the stem, *medic*, then *medic-al, medic-ate, medic-ine*. For *national*, we could point to *nation-ality*, etc.

(ii) Relations between sentence elements. Producing acceptable sentence structure in writing is, to a considerable extent, dependent upon adequate marking of the boundaries of units within the sentence. Yet again, punctuation comes into play as a visual indicator. If we see, for example,

John, the bus conductor was very rude

it may be that John, who is being addressed, is being told that some bus conductor had been rude to the addressor. If, on the other hand, we see

John, the bus conductor, was very rude

we know that a bus conductor called John was rude to some unspecified person. The relation of *bus conductor* to *John* is made clear only by the presence of the comma following *bus conductor*, or by its absence, of course. It is not only phrases which have to be clearly related. It may be letters, words, clauses. And it is not only punctuation which is used to signal the boundaries of the units. If we see

Weneedanicecream

we know that words are there, but are they 'We need an ice cream' or 'We need a nice cream'?

Perhaps the most obvious defects in children's writing occur at clause level. A third-year secondary pupil wrote

When Jen and Maureen had come to the café which was really awful because the people who go there are always fooling about and playing stupid music like Duran Duran.

We see here a string of subordinate clauses and no main clause. Presumably something happened after the girls got to the café, but we are not told, because the awfulness of the café, in the writer's mind, has taken over, and so the chief point of the sentence becomes an expression of distaste for the establishment and its clientele. Neither the point to be made nor the necessary consequent clausal structure has been held securely enough in mind to produce clear relationships between the girls arriving, the awfulness of the café, and the main but unexpressed point which the whole sentence was to have made.

The fact is that units at every level of complexity, from letters to clauses, need to have their relations to each other signified in some way, as expressions of the meaning to be conveyed.

(iii) Cohesion in and between sentences. There are various devices available to enable us to preserve cohesion within a sentence. One is the way we mark agreement between subjects and verbs, so that we write, *the teachers mark books every day* and not, *the teachers marks books every day.* Another is maintaining the agreed conventional sequence of tenses in verb forms. A third is the avoidance of ambiguity in using pronouns; if someone writes, *my father told my brother that the police had telephoned him,* we do not know whether *him* refers to 'my father' or 'my brother'. The kind of grammatical punctuation already referred to is yet another device. Obviously, few people tell themselves when beginning a sentence that they must have regard to devices available for preserving cohesion. It is when things go wrong that conscious, analytic knowledge can help the teacher to help the apprentice writer, the pupil.

To make a text, i.e. a sequence of related sentences, hang together, we need to ensure that cohesion exists between the sentences. Consider the following sequence:

1 It was not so easy as it had seemed at first, to arrange for David to meet Katharine.
2 David himself was the chief impediment.

3   As soon as he had decided to do something, he began to doubt himself.

There is no difficulty in recognizing that those three sentences, taken from a story in a magazine, form part of a coherent text. But if the sequence read:

(a)   As soon as he had decided to do something, he began to doubt himself.
(b)   David himself was the chief impediment.
(c)   It was not so easy as it had seemed at first, to arrange for David to meet Katharine.

all cohesion is lost. In *(a)*, we do not know to whom *he* refers. In *(b)*, we do not know to what David is the chief impediment. In *(c)*, it seems as if a quite new topic is being introduced. We do not need to produce an inventory of all the elements of text cohesion (for a full treatment of cohesion, see Halliday and Hasan 1976, and for a simplified version see Gannon and Czerniewska 1980), but there is no doubt that pupils need to be taught how most clearly to proceed with a text.

It has been possible to mention only one or two instances within each of those areas of concern, but enough has been said to suggest that we keep in mind, in assessing the grammatical features of writing, the following principles:

(i)   Preserve word structure and word order as it is currently accepted in standard English.
(ii)   Indicate the relationships of sentence components so as to produce currently acceptable sentence structure.
(iii)   Preserve cohesion in and between sentences.

If we accept those principles, we can move towards assessing yet another element in pupils' writing, but there are still some pre-requisites of satisfactory assessment. One is that we, as teachers, know enough about the grammar of contemporary English to be able to make rapid, informal analyses of written texts. Another is that we have sufficiently clear expectations concerning the grammars of different kinds of writing. In other words, we must be in a position to consider the grammar of pupils' writing not as an end in itself (that is the concern, and a perfectly proper one, of the linguist) but as another way of carrying meaning.

Shaping a text

If a reader is to be satisfied with a piece of sustained prose, whether it be a story, an account of a scientific experiment, a record of events, or just a paragraph of instructions as to how to get to one place from another, there has to be some 'shape' to it. In other words, there will be an organizational pattern evident within the writing. It is not possible to specify ideal patterns of organization, of course, because the right kind of patterning will depend on the nature of the topic being written about, the form of the genre chosen — letter, magazine article, newspaper column, story for small children — and the readership intended. But some shape there must be, otherwise we end up with a mere sequence of sentences. That, all too often, is what many children produce in school, as any teacher used to marking essays can testify.

Sometimes it is the pupil's fault if a poorly shaped text is handed in, and sometimes it is the teacher's. If a pupil is asked to write without sufficient guidance on what form the writing should take, or without being given sufficient time first to prepare, next to write, then to revise and, if necessary redraft, then it should be no surprise when a loose jumble of sentences lands on the teacher's desk. We shall return to this topic later (see chapter 6), but here, let us consider in a little more detail what we mean by 'shape'.

A story, no matter what its length or nature, will have its structure determined partly by its content, and partly by expectations of order within a story of a given type. If, as is frequently the case, a child's story is a mixture of incident and description (narrative/descriptive in function), we shall expect certain features to be present. We shall expect the sequence of events narrated to be ordered so that they are linked in some comprehensible way. We shall expect some kind of strategy to be adopted for introducing the reader to those events — that is, some kind of recognizable situation. And we shall expect there to be some kind of ending which is not lazy or *ad hoc* (*Then I awoke to find that it had all been a dream*) but which follows from the sequence of events and which by its form as well as content does not leave us turning over the page to find with surprise that the previous line had been the last one after all. Now, these requirements demand of the writer various kinds of organizing ability. One such is the ability to produce the overall or 'external' shape of the piece, while another is to create an 'internal' structure, so that within the story shifts of events are patterned to make sense, in readable 'chunks', and so on. This latter kind of 'internal' patterning is much more amenable to teacher help than the former, since there are teachable skills which can help, such as paragraphing, or being able to use connectives appropriately, or using the process of redrafting (see Thornton 1980, 34−6).

Letter-writing requires a different kind of patterning. Apart from the conventional openings and endings, the purpose of the letter will play an important part in determining the structure. A letter of application for a job, the purpose of which is by nature likely to be persuasive, will be sequenced differently from, and more tightly than, say, a letter responding to a request for advice, which is likely to be more speculative in its content. A letter to a friend describing a holiday will have, or may have, a much looser structure, and will be more discursive. After all, it does not really matter whether you mention the food in the hotel before you complain about your sunburn, or vice versa. The kind of literary critical essay required of older pupils has its own conventions, determined partly by theme or content, but much more by the requirements of the public examination system. (As they change, so we may expect the form of pupils' written work in the later years of secondary schooling to change as well.) All this has implications for the *teaching* of writing rather more than for the *assessment*, but since assessment is part of teaching, we need not be too particular about the distinction.

One of the difficulties of specifying stylistic expectations of written work is the fact that few adults write much at all, and very few write other than for a very restricted purpose, usually for occupational reasons. Adult norms, therefore, tend to be derived from published matter, usually in the form of fiction, but also from non-fiction such as biography, reference material, and ephemeral publications such as newspapers and magazines. Much, then, will depend upon the reading habits of both pupils and teachers as to the nature of the expectations present in any group; one kind of expectation which seems to be common to most classroom teachers of English is that there shall be an extension of word choice in pupils' writing.

'Extension of vocabulary' is a phrase commonly heard in primary schools, but how to help children to extend their repertoires of words is a complex matter. What is certain is that it is not a question of 'learning five new words a day', or committing lists of vocabulary items to memory for tests on Fridays. It is a process of accretion by assimilation, as we read words in a variety of contexts, as we use words in speech and writing, as we enlarge or narrow the contexts of their use, and so gradually increase the size of our active vocabularies. All of us recognize and understand many more words than we actually use, so that our 'passive' vocabularies are much larger than our active ones. Transference from passive to active will come about only if we practise, and see the need to do so. That is why it is encouraging to see a child having recourse to more words, even if inappropriately used, than he has assimilated into his active vocabulary. He is stretching and widening his resources as he does so. It would be foolish, then, to specify criteria for assessing word choice in too strict a manner. But certainly we should be at pains constantly to encourage pupils to choose words accurately from as wide as possible a repertoire.

Literary critics over many centuries have attempted to define style, and to analyse the features of writing deemed to be stylistically impressive. It is not the function of this volume to add to the millions of words already written on the subject, but at the same time it will do no harm to point out that no matter how complex and esoteric the academic arguments have become, in recent years, in discussing style, we are basically concerned with grammatical structure, with organization of thought and material, with effective use of the orthographic uses and conventions of the writing system, and with choice of words.

These, then, are the linguistic features we have very briefly considered in this chapter, and which, when considered in the light of the functions of writing considered in the previous one, can constitute the elements of a framework of assessment, to be considered in the next.

A note on handwriting

The actual graphical substance of writing is quite irrelevant to communicative effectiveness, so long as the alphabetic signs we use in English, i.e. the letters, are distinct. Whether we are reading marks on paper — pencil, ink, print — or electronically transmitted characters on a visual display screen, the important point is that a reader should be able to decipher, without difficulty, the letters which make up the words. Since writing is an individual activity, each child is taught handwriting at school, at first with pencil or crayon and later with ink. It may be that in a few decades children in infant schools will be receiving daily instruction in keyboard procedures, and putting onto VDUs their first attempts to come to terms with the English writing system. Some of us will continue to use fountain pens and 2B pencils. What really matters for effectiveness of communication is that people should have at their command a means for producing signs on a contrasting surface, and that the results should be decipherable. So for the present, at any rate, it is important that children should be taught handwriting that is clear and legible. No more needs to be said here upon the subject.

Summary

1a Spelling is a matter of conforming to a set of standardized conventions. Breaking the conventions need not affect meaning, but it is nonetheless important to observe them as a part of becoming literate.

1b Punctuation is partly a matter of convention and partly a device necessary for conveying meaning.

2a With regard to appropriateness of standard English for written language, there is a difference between what is appropriate, grammatically speaking, and what is correct.

2b We need some guiding principles. We must

- *(i)* preserve word order and word structure
- *(ii)* indicate the relations of sentence components so as to produce acceptable sentence structure
- *(iii)* preserve the cohesion of sentences and between sentences.

3a Texts have to be shaped. The shape will vary according to the nature of the text and according to expectations.

3b Stylistic effectiveness depends on the interaction of: choice of words; grammatical structure; organization of material; use of the orthographic devices and conventions of written English.

4 Handwriting needs to be as legible as other means of written communication.

5
A way of assessing

By far the commonest method of assessing pupils' writing is by 'impression marking'. That is, a teacher takes a piece of writing, reads it, may well make a comment or two in the margin, and at the end makes a fairly rapid decision on what numerical or literal grade should be allotted. There may than follow some summarizing remark. It is not quite such a haphazard process as it sounds when baldly stated, however. In public examinations, analytic mark schemes are frequently used; as mentioned earlier, there is a good deal of research to show that when an analytic scheme is used and the results compared with impression marking of the same scripts by other markers, a fairly high correlation is to be found. So high is the correlation that the language monitoring team of the Assessment of Performance Unit (see References) relies heavily on impression marking for the results of its annual survey of language performance in schools. Those readers familiar with the APU reports on language will already have realized that several of the notions to be found in chapters 3 and 4 are similar to those which underlie the framework of assessment for writing used in those surveys. Since any reasonable method is, to a considerable extent, determined by what is being assessed, that is not surprising. But it should be borne in mind that the APU's techniques were devised for large-scale national sampling rather than for classroom use, so not all the scripts are analytically marked. Approximately 10 per cent are subjected to analytic scrutiny, while all the rest are impression marked, by experience teachers.

If impression marking is so reliable, why then should we bother with anything more complicated? There are several reasons, and four important ones. The first is that while the correlation between impression and analytic marking may be high when we are considering large groups of children, when we are considering only one pupil, things may turn out differently. We cannot, for example, adjust scores to take account of the leniency or stringency of individual markers, nor can we convert raw scores to standardized scores. Second, impressions may or may not be valid – they depend upon the intuitions of the teacher, and teachers, like other people, vary in the reliability of their intuitions. Not all have the relevant experience and/or training. An English teacher may well be trained as a teacher of history or business studies, and be having to fill up a timetable with five or ten periods a week of English teaching, such is the nature of school staffing within our secondary schools. Third, impression marking is rarely diagnostic. It assesses a *product*, but tells little about the *process* of learning to write, during a month, a term, a year. Unless a teacher happens to be particularly interested in, and have some training in, say, grammatical analysis, then aspects of a pupil's writing such as lack of variety in sentence structure, or inaccurate use of pronouns, may go unnoticed (or at least not commented on), so that progress in those areas will be random or, possibly, nonexistent. Fourth, and most important of all, the allotting of an impression mark tends to be thought of as an activity separate from teaching – part of a teacher's duties, certainly, but not quite the same as the flow of activity going on for five or six periods a week with 3D in Room Z. It is what gets done at home, or in the staffroom, or on the bus. (That is not meant to be flippant or dismissive. The sheer quantity of work that has to be read by teachers is very large.)

It is useful for teachers to build up a cumulative record of children's progress in acquiring writing skills; the compiling of such a record is part of the teacher's task, while children are given the opportunities to write for a variety of purposes; part of that continuing assessment should be a consideration of how well pupils are progressing in respect of mastery of the features of language mentioned in chapter 4. It should be stressed here that children's performance in writing is, to a significant extent, 'task-specific'. One of the most interesting findings of the surveys carried out by the Assessment of Performance Unit is that pupils vary in their use of linguistic skills according to the nature of the writing task. That is, the language used is to some extent determined by the purpose, the theme, and the readership of the writing undertaken, as well as by the interest and motivation of the writer. So progress in mastery of writing skills should be seen in relation to the types of tasks undertaken, and not merely as a step-by-step movement up a slope of linguistic competence, without reference to what, why and for whom texts are written. If viewed in this contextually determined light, then assessment can legitimately be seen as a continuous and continuing process of diagnosis, encouraging of strengths, remediation of error, and, in an ever widening range of writing functions, further diagnosis.

Records must be kept if the process is to be a continuing one, and it is not difficult to build up an informal profile of a pupil's progress by the use of charts such as those represented in figures 1 and 2 (pp. 64 and 66). It is not suggested that every piece of writing by every pupil be analytically scrutinized. But if, in a class of 30 pupils, five scripts are subjected to fairly detailed examination every week, then in the space of a year, a useful file could be compiled for every member of the class — the value of the file residing not in its final content, but rather in the use made of it during that time and in succeeding years. A sheet of the kind represented in figure 1 could be completed for each piece of work assessed; a further chart could be kept for each pupil (see figure 2) so that a cumulative record could be built up.

The chart in figure 1 could be used in the following way. Details of the specific task set and to be assessed would be entered, e.g. 'A story suitable for reading to primary school children or to first year secondary pupils', together with what led up to the task, and in what context it had been set, e.g. 'from reading of mythical/legendary tales over past two weeks, and following discussion of qualities likely to appeal to different readerships'. The function of the writing, in terms of the types outlined in chapter 3, would also appear — in the case of the examples given, 'narrative/descriptive', (or either). Then comments under the different headings at A-F could appear, the headings reflecting the concerns mentioned in chapter 4. (See Appendix to this chapter, pp. 75–8, for further comments.) A general, overall comment could be entered at the bottom, if so desired, with any points thought to be worth noting for later reference.

It would not be difficult to relate to the comments under each heading some numerical score, if the teacher wished to do that. For example, a score on a rising scale from 1–6 would not be too difficult to assign, for each of the spaces numbered 1–10 at the right hand side of the sheet. It does not really matter what scale is used, so long as the scoring is consistent and the scale is short. To achieve consistency, it is plainly necessary to have in mind some criteria, however informally they may be expressed. Under some of the

NAME:	DATE:	

WRITTEN TASK ASSIGNED:

CONTEXT/PREPARATION:

FUNCTION:

A	SHAPING OF TEXT: (i) OVERALL STRUCTURE:	1
	(ii) ORGANIZATION OF CONTENT:	2
B	VOCABULARY: (i) APPROPRIATENESS:	3
	(ii) VARIETY:	4
C	GRAMMATICAL FEATURES: (i) WORD STRUCTURE AND WORD ORDER:	5
	(ii) SENTENCE STRUCTURE:	6
	(iii) COHESION IN/BETWEEN SENTENCES:	7
D	SPELLING:	8
E	PUNCTUATION:	9
F	ORIGINALITY AND APPROPRIATENESS OF CONTENT:	10

GENERAL:	FOLLOW-UP:

Figure 1   Task assessment sheet

headings, the criteria will be the same for every task, and under others, different criteria will apply to different functions and different tasks. Obviously, the overall structure of a story has to be judged rather differently from that of a piece describing the principles and operation of an internal combustion engine. Other factors will remain more constant. At C, for instance, the resources available to a pupil in respect of sentence structure are determined not so much by the task, and not only by the pupil's ability, but by the nature of the language itself; at D, few choices are open to anyone for spelling, rather more at E, for punctuation, but both aspects are generally fairly easy to specify, and to evaluate in practice.

The scale needs to be short for two reasons. First, while it is not too difficult to specify a limited number of criteria, it becomes both difficult and unwieldy to multiply distinctions over a long scale. Second, the aim is not to arrange a rank order for numbers of individuals. If you were doing that you might wish to use the usual percentage scores (though I doubt whether there has ever been much difference worth considering between a piece of work scoring 57 per cent and 59 per cent), but here all that is needed is a mnemonic, as it were, so that on assessment of the next task to be performed, one can quickly see what differences, improvements, etc. may have appeared. It is better to have a scale with even numbers, so that the temptation to plump for the middle, in the case of indecision, is avoided; that is why a six-point rather than a seven-point scale is suggested. An appendix to this chapter suggests kinds of criteria for each of sections A-F.

If numerical scores were assigned, they could be entered into the pupil record as displayed in figure 2. The roman numerals in the first column refer to the types of writing completed, i.e. the six functions discussed in pp. 44−7 above, while the next column merely provides spaces for five different entries for each function. The following ten columns refer to the ten scores entered the task assessment sheet.

We can see how this works out in practice by considering a piece of writing completed by a pupil. The procedures outlined above and in previous chapters may be applied to writing performed by pupils of any age, but the text reproduced below, which we shall consider, was written by an 11-year-old, and is not untypical of the kind of writing produced by many children either at the end of the primary phase of school or at the beginning of the secondary phase. (Lines have been numbered for ease of reference.)

NAME: _____

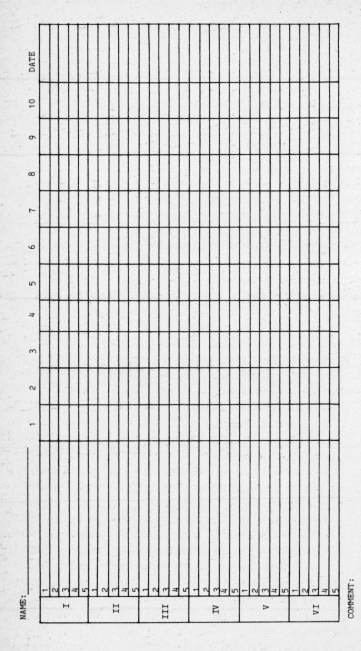

Figure 2 Pupil record sheet (writing)

COMMENT:

Neighbours

1 I have been living in a new house since 17th December.
2 I have not met my two neighbours. They have been moving in and
3 out but have not spoken to me. The neighbours on my left have
4 a dog. It is some kind of a collie. The people on my right
5 have a grey poodle. They also have a daughter who is supposed
6 to be 10 but she looks about 13. My neighbour in school is Stan
7 he is tall his age is 11 but he looks 6 and makes faces like a
8 2 year old. Stephen stis left to me he is 9 usually aggravating
9 spiteful but genrally cheerful. A lady with ginger hair lives
10 a couple of doors away at No. 13. Before we moved in she came
11 over to us and began asking personal questions. I at once
12 nicknamed her, 'Nosey Ginger nut.' The neighbours at my other
13 house were liked very much by me. Billy sits oppisite but
14 the thing I would like to say would be disliked by my teacher.

(Chris − aged 11)

It is clearly not possible to re-create the context in which this piece was written and set − that is, to know what work had been done by Chris and the other members of the class during the term, what the relations with the teacher were like, exactly how much discussion had taken place, what help had been given during the process of composing the piece, and so on. However, allowing for that, it seems as if Chris has not been clear enough in her mind (or his? Readers may care to think about what sex they had already ascribed to Chris) about what was needed. The topic of neighbours has been very broadly interpreted, at any rate. The task was set following a discussion, and it was envisaged that the group should write on the theme of 'neighbours' from a personal point of view, saying what pleased or displeased them, what the attributes of good and bad neighbours should be, etc. What we have here is a set of 15 sentences, loosely connected by the characters mentioned being, or having been, in different ways, in a state of physical proximity to the writer.

As for the shaping of the text, overall it is very loosely planned. We have six sentences on the people who live on either side of the writer's house, then we switch to the two classmates who sit either side of her in the classroom, before moving back to another and disliked domestic neighbour. After a parenthetic comment on some previous neighbours, we end with a further remark on a classmate. However, there is *some* organizing ability here. The opening is entirely appropriate as following from the title of the piece; then there is an obvious but worthwhile symmetry in the treatment first of the neighbours living on either side, and second of the two boys who sit on either side. If the passage had been paragraphed in layout, even though only according to the house/classroom settings, so that paragraph 2 began at line 6, 'My neighbour in school . . .', with a third paragraph at line 9, 'A lady with . . .', and a fourth at line 13, 'Billy . . .' then the piece as a whole might have been seen to have had a more deliberated structure than was probably the case. The passage as a whole has only a minimally appropriate shape, and on a rising scale of $1-6$, it could be assigned only a rather low score.

As for vocabulary, there is evidence in the text of a sense of the need to adapt word choice to the mode of written, as distinct from spoken, discourse, e.g. in the avoidance of contractions such as *haven't* for *have not*, or writing *at once* for *straightway* or *straight-away*. There is also an attempt to produce the kind of cumulative description common to some kinds of writing, such as those found in popular newspapers, as, for example, in ll. $8-9$, where Stephen is described as *usually aggravating spiteful but genrally cheerful*. (The errors here lie in lack of punctuation, spelling, and omission of *and* before 'spiteful'.) Apart from that, the vocabulary is competently neutral, but with sufficient variety to avoid monotony. There is, too, a brief instance of dry humour in l. 5, where a daughter is added to the canine possessions of the neighbours, and the use of *supposed* in referring to the daughter's age.

What of the grammar? As far as word structure is concerned, Chris displays a good deal of competence. She has no difficulty in coping with many words which cause trouble to pupils of her age. We may note that words such as *aggravating, spiteful, personal*, cause no problem. The two items which stand out are, of course, *genrally* and *oppisite*, but these are best dealt with under spelling. Similarly, the only points concerning word order, which occur in the last two sentences, are better dealt with under the heading of sentence structure.

If we consider the sentence structure, the first thing to notice is that it is, on the whole, fairly simple. By 'simple', I mean a structure consisting of little more than the form, subject (S) + verb (V) + object (O) or some form of adverbial complement, or an adjunct of some sort (A). The first six sentences have the following structure:

1 S V A A
2 S V O
3 S V A + *but* + V A
4 S V O
5 S V O
6 S V O

The next sentence (l. 5) is more complex, but is faulty. It has the basic form S V O, but the object, *daughter*, is then modified by *who is supposed to be 10 but she looks about 13*. The sentence would have been better recast as either

who is supposed to be 10 but looks about 13

or

who is supposed to be 10, although she looks about 13

Chris has not yet appreciated that, when a pronoun is the subject of a sentence (*who* in *who is supposed*), if a second verb follows (*looks*), then either we repeat the pronoun or omit a second subject altogether; we do not use a different pronoun (*she*). If we introduce some sort of conjunction such as *although*, we can more easily introduce another subject, even if that other subject takes the form of a pronoun referring to the same person. The next sentence (ll. 6–8) is ill-punctuated, for it consists really of three separable sentences

1 My neighbour in school is Stan
2 He is tall
3 His age is 11, but he looks 6 and makes faces like a 2 year old.

He is tall would have been better if introduced as a relative clause *who is tall*, with the following clauses recast, to give us *My neighbour in school is Stan, who is tall and aged 11, though he looks 6 and makes faces like a 2 year old*. There is nothing wrong with the basic grammatical patterns of Chris's writing here. It is merely that she has failed to mark properly the sentence boundaries. The same occurs in the next sentence, which really consists of two sentences –

1 Stephen stis (i.e. sits) left to me
2 He is 9 . . . cheerful.

In this sentence, there is also the deviant *left to me*, for *on my left*. Little of note, grammatically speaking, then occurs until the last two sentences, where passive verb forms have been used instead of the more usual and, in this case, more appropriate active forms. It is possible that the reason for the use of the passive is the prominence in the writer's mind of the notion of neighbours. This, after all, is the theme of the passage, and turned into the subject of the sentence, as it is when the passive voice is used, it gains prominence. We might also notice that *at my other house* very awkwardly modifies *The neighbours*. It was not the neighbours who were at the other house, but the writer herself, and so *at my other house* should really be modifying *I*, which does not occur in the sentence as written. Had Chris taken these points into account, the sentence might have emerged as *I very much liked my neighbours when I lived at our other house*, but either she did not think of that kind of structure, or felt that some more emphatic − or at least different − structure was called for. Similarly, in the final sentence, it is very probable that the thing uppermost in her mind was what she had really wanted to say about Billy, and so *the thing I would like to say* is brought forward to the front of the sentence as subject. It may also have been that to have written *Billy sits opposite to me but my teacher would dislike the thing I would like to say about him* was thought to be too direct a comment on the teacher! Children very quickly learn the desirability of linguistic tact in their transactions with adults, especially at school.

The cohesion of the passage is competently handled. Apart from the sentence beginning in l. 5, (*They also have a daughter*) the sentences of the passage are not marred by any lack of internal cohesion. Pronouns are used competently and without ambiguity, and although a jarring effect is created by the alternation of comment on neighbours at home and that on neighbours at school, there is no confusion or ambiguity relating to what or who is being referred to. It is the overall structure of the content of the piece that is odd, not the means used to express it.

What immediately catch the eye, on a first reading of the piece, are the orthographic features. There are three spelling errors − *stis* (1.8), *genrally* (1.9), *oppisite* (1.13). The *stis* sequence of letters, for *sits*, is presumably a simple case of transposition of the letters *i* and *t*, and merely pointing out to the writer that *stis* should have been written *sits* would have taken care of that 'slip of the pen' — since Chris writes the word perfectly correctly in l. 13. The two items *genrally* and *oppisite* are rather different. Matters of spelling frequently overlap with other aspects of language, and mis-spellings are often indicators of trouble with areas of language structure. It might well be the case here that more accurate representations of word structure could be achieved by the writer if the teacher were to introduce lists of related words (see Thornton 1980, 42−45; Stubbs 1980, 60; Keen 1978, 78). It is frequently useful to point to different stress patterns in pronunciation, when grouping together related words, so that mis-spellings are thrown into prominence. For example, in the case of *generally*, it would be useful to compare

> *generally*　　with *generálity*
> (see p. 54
> 　above)　　　　etc.

The same applies here to *oppisite*, where words such as *oppose* or *opposing* might be drawn to the pupil's attention.

The punctuation of the passage is relatively free from error, but note should be taken of the four occasions where it does go astray. In ll. 6−7, the sentence starting *My neighbour at school* . . . twice omits the conventional full stop + capital letter which mark a sentence boundary in English. The same thing happens in the following sentence, and in this one there is also the omission of commas following the adjectives *aggravating* and *spiteful*. Two minor errors occur in l. 10, where we might expect a comma after *nicknamed her*. The fact that there are no other errors is to some extent dependent upon the relative simplicity of the sentence structure, especially in the first six lines.

Looking back over the passage as a whole, we may wish to consider the general content, the *what* is said, as distinct from the *how* it is said. Not all writing tasks demand originality of content. Indeed, some preclude it, as, for example, the relaying of instructions, or a factual record of events. It is, moreover, unrealistic to expect much originality of content or style from an 11-year-old, who has a difficult job to do in achieving any kind of writing fluency. However, in considering the content of the writing, the appropriateness of what is said to the given theme, and its interest, we are forced to say that Chris's material does not rise above mere factual statement in relation to the neighbours mentioned — dogs owned by them, ages of classmates, colour of the lady's hair, etc. There is little beyond that, except in the middle (ll. 7–9, as already mentioned) and at the end, in the final, primly daring implication about the teacher and the intriguing Billy.

Now, a great deal depends upon the presentation and preparation of any writing task. Was 'Neighbours' presented simply as a title, even allowing for the fact that some discussion had taken place? What genre of writing was requested or suggested? Was it to be a story for a class magazine, a dialogue, a diary entry, a complaint, a letter? The likelihood is that relatively little attention was given to this aspect of the task. Unless a good deal of time is given to a consideration of what kind of writing is being asked for, the task tends to be too generalized, and rests on no explicit model of writing styles or functions. Would Chris have produced a more original, better structured piece if she had had longer to consider, in a group of pupils, different ways of presenting material for specific purposes, and had had some explicit knowledge of different styles, had drafted a piece for discussion, correction (perhaps by fellow members of her group), redrafting, and time in which to reconsider and rewrite? Almost certainly, yes.

But let us draw together our impressions and judgements, and try to record them in some informal fashion, by using the simple assessment sheets. A shorthand assessment of Chris's piece then might look like figure 3. There are several things to note about this sheet. First, we have had to enter some entirely speculative comment, as at 'General' and at 'Follow up,' for example. This is because any piece of work assessed should be within a context, and we have had to make up a context, with regard to a previous assessment (General) and to a putative teacher's notions for continuing with Chris's development as a writer. It is important to stress yet again that we are not suggesting that any kind of mechanistic process involving box-ticking, reductionist aide-memoires, or even profile charts, will help children to write better. Only the child and the teacher working together can effect improvement. But by regularly looking in detail at the writing of each pupil in a class, constructing a picture, however, crude, of areas of strengths and weaknesses, and recording them for future reference and action, we might be able to do more than just mark in red every error on a piece of writing, thereby demoralizing the pupil, tiring ourselves, and merely filling up the columns of a mark book.

It will be noticed that no overall or general grading has been given to 'Neighbours'. It is difficult to see why any should be given.

NAME: **Chris**   DATE: **1.4.84**

WRITTEN TASK ASSIGNED: **Neighbours** - what sort of people, what you like
and dislike about neighbours, what makes good and bad neighbours.
CONTEXT/PREPARATION: Following discussion on what pleases and annoys you
about people close to you.

FUNCTION: Narrative/descriptive.

	SHAPING OF TEXT:		
A	(i) OVERALL STRUCTURE: Starts well, but then tends to wander about. The piece as a whole has no organized shape, and there is no discernible ending.	1	2
	(ii) ORGANIZATION OF CONTENT: Comments on neighbours at home have been mixed with neighbours in class. Each part's elements seem random and have little to do with assigned topic (cf. dogs, ages, and appearance). Only at end is there a personal address to the theme.	2	2
	VOCABULARY:		
B	(i) APPROPRIATENESS: Generally appropriate for unspecified readership. Has paid some attention to written forms - limited	3	4
	(ii) VARIETY: Some attempt made to assign attributes by E. to characters mentioned by use of adjectives appropriately used. Is able to specify items by appropriate nouns (collie, poodle).	4	4
	GRAMMATICAL FEATURES:		
C	(i) WORD STRUCTURE AND WORD ORDER: Quite competent.	5	6
	(ii) SENTENCE STRUCTURE: Moderate only - when complex sentences attempted (only three), faulty arrangement of clauses. Inappropriate use of passive voice.	6	3
	(iii) COHESION IN/BETWEEN SENTENCES: Fair - but because of poor organization of material the text does not cohere. Faults semantic rather than grammatical - needs more pre-planning.	7	4
D	SPELLING: Quite good, only three errors. One accidental, other two relate to unstressed vowel sounds.	8	5
E	PUNCTUATION: (a) falls down in relation to sentence structure; (b) needs surer use of comma to separate sentence elements; full stop as sentence boundary marker.	9	4
F	ORIGINALITY AND APPROPRIATENESS OF CONTENT: Little originality evident - nothing on attributes of good/bad neighbours. Some effort made to express reactions.	10	2

GENERAL: Encouraging improvement in spelling - progress since 6.2.84, but still poorly organized and does not seem happy with more abstract topics.

FOLLOW-UP: (a) Practice in organizing material - need for planning (more note-form tasks?). (b) Use of punctuation to signal boundaries. (c) Experiment with more adventurous sentence structure (different reading? specific exercises?).

Figure 3   Completed task assessment sheet

What is important is comparing performances by the same pupil over a range of writing tasks in different areas of 'writing behaviour' as it were, and with reference to different aspects of language — orthography, grammar, word choice, etc. It would not be difficult, of course, to assign a mark out of 10, or 20, or 100, or whatever. But what for? That is one of the most important questions we can ask ourselves before setting a piece of work, before marking it, before handing it back, before talking about it, and before recording any moment assigned. Of course, if one were to give up assigning general scores in favour of scrutinizing in detail different aspects of language and language use, then the rationale underlying changes in classroom procedure would have to be justified to many people (see Thornton 1980, 66, and chapter 6 below), but no one except the ignorant ever pretended that teaching is easy.

Appendix to chapter 5

Examples of informal criteria for A-F of task assessment sheet (figure 1, p. 64)

A Shaping of a text

It is not appropriate to separate different criteria for the overall structure and for the organization of the content. The second will depend to a considerable extent upon the first, and, apart from the control of material within a paragraph, will be determined by such extralinguistic factors as knowledge, motivation and preparation. For the general purpose of assessing the 'shape' of a piece of writing, however, it is as well to have in mind some generalized criteria of the following kind, in which the figures denote the points on a six-point scale of performance. The (by now) familiar *caveat* must be entered; different tasks will yield different responses from the same individual. 'Appropriateness' refers to the task-specific shape of the writing.

6 Clear and appropriate overall structure, with content arranged in a way which satisfies adult readers' expectations for the age of the writer. Indications of opening and closing, where relevant. Clear paragraphing where relevant.

5 Clear and appropriate overall structure, with opening and closing where relevant. Content arranged in such a way as to avoid confusion, though may have rather loose paragraphing, or other weakness of organizational structure within the text.

4 Discernible overall structure, even if openings and/or endings are weak, and without gross imbalance of organizational structure.

3 Poor overall structure, e.g. no discernible ending, but without confusion arising from nonetheless faulty arrangement within the text.

2 Poor overall structure, with poor arrangement of text material.

1 No apparent structure, either overall or within the text.

Note that no pupil would be given a zero mark, unless he had not written anything at all. If zero is included, we are effectively using a seven-point scale.

B Vocabulary

6 Wide vocabulary, appropriate to the topic or theme, and to the readership, with no carelessly or insensitively chosen words, and vocabulary suited to theme and readership.

5 Use of appropriately chosen words, with only one or two instances in the text of faulty choice, in a reasonably extensive vocabulary free from undue repetition.

4 Generally appropriate vocabulary, with some evidence of successful matching of word choice to readership and theme, despite instances of repetition and/or inaccurate reference (e.g. *infer* for *imply* in the writing of older pupils), or lack of specificity, e.g. *thing* for a more appropriately specific noun.

3 Some inappropriate word choices and little evidence of success in matching vocabulary to topic; repetition, lack of accuracy, false senses implied.

2 Generally inappropriate and narrow vocabulary, e.g. large numbers of colloquialisms in a piece where a more impersonal style is required. Use of spoken idioms.

1 Meagre, and/or totally inappropriate vocabulary.

C Grammatical features
(i) Word structure and word order

6 Effective word structure and word order, free from error. Where deviations from standard forms occur, they are for clear stylistic purposes.

5 Adequate structure and order, generally free from error.

4 Adequate word order with a sprinkling of errors in word structure, e.g. inaccurate use of prefixes, or suffixes, misrepresentation of spoken syllabic structure (other than by mere

mis-spelling).

3 Occasional faulty word order, e.g. in verb phrases or placing of adverbial phrases, with errors of word structure.

2 Faults in both word order and word structure throughout the text.

1 Totally inadequate.

(ii) Sentence structure

6 Showing a command of sentence structure with a range of complexity and variety of structure to match theme, readership, and stylistic demands of genre.

5 Showing a command of different sentence structures, but with less certainty than at level 6, e.g. faulty sequences of tense after parentheses, or repetition of similar structures where variety would be desirable.

4 Adequate command of sentence structures used, but with limited variety and occasional faults.

3 Faults in complex sentence structure; repetition of simple sentences even where inappropriate.

2 Simple (i.e. S V (O) (A)) sentences with occasional errors.

1 Generally faulty structure, even in simple sentences.

(iii) Cohesion

6 Sentences relate to each other, with good use of connectives; correct use of pronouns in inter-sentential reference, and no ambiguity within sentences.

5 Occasional lapses into ambiguity within sentences, or lack of clear sequencing of sentences.

4 Fair cohesion between sentences, but poor use of connectives, poor pronoun reference, and ambiguity.

3 Disconnected sentences, with persistent instances of ambiguity or lack of clarity both within and between sentences.

2 Poor cohesion throughout.

1 Complete absence of cohesion — random sentences written in lieu of a text.

D Spelling

6 Free from error.

5 Generally free from error, with the occasional lapse, other

than the obvious 'slip of the pen'.

4 Evidence of some systematic, as opposed to random, mis-spelling.

3 Frequent and systematic mis-spelling.

2 Constant mis-spellings, even of simple words which most pupils of similar age can spell correctly.

1 Total failure to assimilate spelling conventions of English.

E Punctuation

6 Free from error, and displaying command of punctuation conventions in addition to full stop, comma, direct speech punctuation, and capitalization.

5 No errors in grammatical punctuation, with only the occasional omission or error in other cases.

4 Occasional errors which result in ambiguity or lack of clarity, e.g. sentence boundary markers.

3 Persistent errors, but ones which do not lead to structural ambiguity.

2 Gross incidence of error which leads to structural ambiguity.

1 Total failure to assimilate punctuation conventions of English.

F Originality

No criteria are given for originality, since at this point we have reached the limits of assessability. It is, of course, possible to distinguish between the wholly derivative and that which stands out as unique to the individual, but the subjectivity of both teacher and pupil play such a large role in assessing what is and is not original that it would be pointless to suggest criteria. That does not make it impossible for a specific teacher assessing a specific pupil to assign some point on a scale, of course; it is for the individual teacher to decide, with a knowledge of the pupil being assessed, how (or, indeed, whether) to evaluate this aspect of the writing.

6
Some implications for classroom organization

What action is taken by a teacher with regard to any aspect of curriculum development depends very much on the professional position held. The class teacher, the inspector, the head of department, the adviser, the head of school — each has different functions. The matter of this chapter relates, for the most part, to the teacher in the classroom. Since we are not in the business of prescribing, but rather, in accordance with the title of this series, of exploring, we shall also be selective; guided by what has been said in the foregoing chapters, there are three major areas to be considered, then, relating to range of writing purposes, language structure, and, since assessment is part of teaching, some implications for teaching.

Range of purposes

If children are to practise writing for as wide as possible a range of purposes, this has implications beyond those relating to what they are required to write. In a book on the nature of writing, one would have to consider the relationships between speaking and writing, between writing and reading, and how the interrelationships affect the development of each. That is not the purpose here, but it is important to consider some of the effects of the way the different modes of language activity interact.

There is little doubt that the provision of exemplars, in any human activity, can be influential. Obviously, a great deal depends upon motivation, and the importance set upon the social values underlying the exemplars. This is evident, and most obviously so, in the dress, speech habits, and leisure preoccupations of teenagers. What is seen by teenagers in the habits of their popstar exemplars is frequently adopted, sartorially and verbally, with a fierce conformism. In the wider world outside school, people's writing habits are, to some extent, fashioned by their reading habits, i.e. by the models they derive from exemplars. Since this applies as much to school pupils as to anyone and since it is part of a teacher's job partly to fashion their habits, it follows that in the teaching of writing we need to pay attention to the reading habits fostered. A wide range of writing implies the coexistence of a wide range of reading. Teachers who wish to assess pupils' writing constructively, in the context of *teaching* writing, should, then, have a notion of language development going well beyond the limits of a public examination or a class coursebook.

Following from the above is a further implication concerned with preparation. A wide range of writing and reading demands an overview of the teaching and learning programme which, though it cannot be specified in advance, must, it is clear, stretch over more than a week, or a month, or a term. It demands selection and preparation of material which take into account more than *theme* or *content*. Specifying a topic for a class over a term or half a term on, say, 'fantasy', needs more than a hunt for tales and poems of fantasy. It needs the provision of different kinds of writing tasks, and different kinds of written exemplars, which will involve recording, explanation, narrative etc. The marking of work issuing from a thematic approach will sometimes demand the ignoring of the topic for the sake of concentrating on a particular linguistic aspect of the writing, just as consideration of the formal features of writing may sometimes be ignored for the sake of focussing on the way the material is organized (in so far as different aspects *can* be separated). This in turn may require a reordering of material throughout a term, for specific purposes and for different pupils.

But it is not just the assigning of a range of tasks which promotes writing for different purposes. The readership, too, has to be considered. It is difficult, and time-consuming, to devise situations where the readership of a pupil's writing is other than oneself, the teacher. But it should be attempted. If a letter is to be written, it can be to a known recipient other than the teacher; if a story is to be written, it can be for a predetermined readership, such as a different class, or children in a different school; if a piece of factual recording is to be completed it can be for another teacher or group of teachers in school. Parents, local employers, local authority advisers, all can be used, with requisite measures of tact, persuasion, and ingenuity, to provide 'real life' readerships or audiences for classroom writing.

Language structure

If we are to consider the structural components of writing, then a major implication is that 'knowledge of and about language must form part of the English teacher's equipment for the job' (Thornton 1980, 64–5). It is still a matter of regret that only a minority of English teachers have pursued any substantial course of study, either in initial training or later, of the structural and functional workings of their mother-tongue. Many other writers (notably of books in this series) have commented upon this point, and there is no need to pursue it further.

A more practical implication is concerned with what happens to the bulk of prose produced in any given week by the 20 or 30 pupils in a class. As mentioned in the previous chapter, it is not envisaged that every bit of writing shall be subjected to detailed scrutiny. What happens between the six- or eight-weekly detailed assessments? Well, first there should be far less general marking. There is no need to mark everything, for a start. Indeed, if drafting and redrafting are to be normal features of learning to write, it would be absurd to mark everything written. And, when a piece is marked, not all linguistic features need to be regarded simultaneously. Marking could be much more selective than it usually is; there is no good reason why pupils should not know that this or that particular piece of writing is to be looked at from the point of view of only one feature, such as sentence structure, paragraphing or spelling. If more than one feature is to be considered, there is no imperative reason why part of a text should not be read for one feature and part for another. Obviously, the whole piece has to be *read* by the teacher, in order to judge how well the text has been shaped and how well the content has been arranged. But the covering of scripts in red ink should give way to a much more selective approach. There is no good reason, too, why the teacher has to be the only person to mark, if what is to be marked does not demand an expert technical knowledge. Some things cannot be left to pupils, and there is no getting around the fact that English teachers will always have to spend many hours on texts; but children themselves can be the most ruthless of copy editors when it comes to checking, for example, spelling of each others' work.

The main point is that regardless of how we go about it, we ought to concern ourselves with pupils' use of language at different linguistic levels. By *levels* is meant the different stages of complexity at which units of language operate.

So, at the highest level we have a text. The text consists of units at a lower level, which may be chapters, or episodes; and those − or the text itself − will consist of paragraphs and so on; paragraphs consist of sentences; a sentence consists of clauses; a clause consists of phrases; a phrase consists of words; and words consist of letters. We shall have to attend in the classroom to all of those levels of language units, but not necessarily all at the same time.

Organization

Just as it is unnecessary to consider simultaneously all the facets of language used in a pupil's text, so not all pupils will need to focus their attention on the same things at the same time. There needs to be a grouping of pupils for the purposes of assessment (and some groups may, of course, comprise only a single pupil). But if a cumulative record, however informal, is built up of a pupil's writng skills, it need not take too long to recognize loose groupings within the class on the basis of need for work at different levels of language complexity. This does not mean that every pupil always has to perform an individual task. What it means is that in marking the work of a group of 25 pupils, a teacher may in practice be marking five or six sets of five or six papers each, and focussing on a different aspect of writing performance for each set.

If, for example, half a dozen pupils are consistently restricting themselves to the simplest sentence patterns with the monotonous repetition of simple conjunctions − *I walked down the street and I saw my friend and we went to the café and then we . . .* etc. − it might be more profitable to skim over any other issues in order to induce the writers to experiment with more complex patterns, in order to achieve greater effectiveness. Now that could become very sterile if approached abstractly, by talking to pupils in terms of structures. If, however, a pupil is writing a chronologically sequential set of events, the teacher might suggest that instead of writing *I got up and then I had breakfast and then I went out and then . . .*, the pupil could consider different ways of expressing temporal progression such as *After getting up, I had my breakfast and . . .*, or *When I had got up and had had my breakfast, I . . .*, etc. If the practice of grammatical subordination can be undertaken in relation to a meaning, and within a context, there is a much better chance that subordinate structures will be assimilated into the pupil's stylistic repertoire than if abstract rules are presented, to be learned but never used.

No-one is suggesting, of course, that an increase in grammatical complexity necessarily means an increase in effectiveness. We can all think of extremely complex structures in language which are so dense as to be almost totally ineffective — just think of official forms, such as your tax returns; often even worse are the guides to official forms, which are so complex as to be almost completely unintelligible. No, the relationship between complexity and choice is less direct. The latter exists for a writer when he is able to *make choices* from among a wide repertoire of structures in order to achieve the desired effect. That implies an *ability* to use complex structures, not the *necessity* for using them. This reinforces the first aspect mentioned in this chapter — the necessity for providing contexts for a wide range of language uses.

By concentrating on constructive approaches to children's writing rather than simply marking errors, we have a better chance of helping our pupils to improve their writing performance than if we simply rely on uncontextualized exercises or on coursebooks, which cannot take into account individual difficulties, weaknesses and strengths. This applies to every level of language structure, whether we are dealing with the structure of a word, or of a phrase, clause, sentence, paragraph, or with whole-text structures. The requisites for success are:

(a) sufficient knowledge on the part of the teacher; and
(b) a contextualization of different structures, so that pupils see that there is some point in learning what a teacher wants them to learn.

What then of the teacher in the classroom with perhaps five teaching groups every week, 150 or so individual children to meet, and an ever-present marking load? Previous chapters do not set out to say anything about how to teach, except indirectly and occasionally. Clearly, however, if assessment is part of teaching, as has frequently been repeated, then we have to consider some aspects of teaching methods. The first is that there must be group teaching as distinct from whole-class teaching. Not all the time, not necessarily every day, but when it is necessary in order to introduce new topics to those pupils who need them, or for them to practise techniques recently acquired. It is extremely unlikely that in a class of 25 or 30, every pupil will simultaneously be at the same point in the progression towards literacy.

There is nothing intrinsically good or bad about class teaching, group teaching, or individual teaching. All depends on what is being taught, to whom and for what purpose. How teaching is carried on will depend to some extent on what your personal view of teaching is. If, like the present writer, you believe that education is essentially an activity involving three elements — teacher, pupil and subject matter — with all three elements inseparable each from the others, then you will almost inevitably be led to a variety of techniques. If you know that no pupil in your class has had any previous experience of writing, say, expository argument, then there is no good reason for not teaching the whole class as a class. When it comes to writing imaginative prose, it may well be that four or five pupils have previously displayed exceptional talent in that area; for those pupils, the chief need is time. But it may be useful to split up the rest of the class into three or four groups, each writing within a different context and towards different ends. In any class, in any school, there is always a very wide range of ability, and of experience. If we are going to assess writing performance constructively, then it will be necessary to judge pupils' work with a consideration of their different experiences, abilities and rates of progression in relation to whichever aspect of writing is being acquired, developed or improved.

For pupils to be able to benefit in the ways mentioned, each will need, on a regular basis, the individual attention of his or her teacher, even if only for a few minutes. This is entirely possible, but it needs a degree of organization at departmental and preferably school level. There is nothing permanently valid in the notion of 'a class'. Given the will, and a moderately flexible timetable, most English departments can — and some do — alter groupings of pupils, to allow teachers to spend one or two periods a week with no more than half a dozen pupils. There are several ways of organizing the possibility of every pupil's regularly receiving for a short time the undivided attention of a teacher. Admittedly, it is difficult to do this unless both the head of department and head of school are agreeable, and so will frame the timetable in a way that will allow it; where such agreement does not exist, it has to be argued and pleaded for.

The force of arguments adduced to effect change needs to be

based on teachers' knowledge and conviction. Unfortunately, there still exists a good deal of misunderstanding within our schools of the nature and functions of language. This is partly because few initial teacher training courses contain a substantial and coherent course on language; partly it is because of serving teachers' inability, or disinclination, to remedy that deficiency. For those who believe that course book exercises will initiate learning, that explicit knowledge of the structure and functioning of language is irrelevant, that children will improve their writing performance without sharp assessment — for all of those, in-service training is necessary. Where no in-service training is possible, either through difficulties of obtaining secondment or inadequate provision in a local authority area, a useful start could be made by any individual teacher through systematic reading. A useful reading list might have, as its basis, the references marked with an asterisk in this volume.

In this brief volume, certain assumptions have been made; some of those assumptions are familiar to anyone who has read earlier books in the series, while others may be less so. Among the more important of these assumptions are:

(i)   that education is a process involving a three-way relationship between teachers, pupil, and subject matter, and therefore that what teachers know and do matters.

(ii) that for a teacher of English, a knowledge of the nature, structure and functioning of the English language is necessary.

(iii) that raising of levels of performance in writing is best brought about by extending the range of tasks set to involve as wide as possible a variety of purposes for writing.

(iv) that systematic assessment is inherent in and essential to good teaching.

(v)   That assessment, in whatever form adopted, should be recorded, and used for the purposes of diagnosis, remediation, and improvement.

Those who share a belief in these assumptions may have their own methods; those who do not may care to consider some of the notions advanced, together with the consequences for their own work; of those who are seeking to help children in schools to write better than they already do, few will rest content with the present widespread practice, in marking written work, of concentration upon surface error. It is neither possible nor desirable to specifiy a 'right way' of refining our methods, but for those who have yet to develop an approach, it may be that the present contribution will assist.

References

(An asterisk denotes a book or article which might usefully be taken as a starting point for further reading.)

BRITTON, J. 1970: *Language and learning*. London: Allen Lane The Penguin Press.

*BROOKES, A. and HUDSON, R. 1982: Do linguists have anything to say to teachers? In Carter 1982.

BROWN, G. and YULE, G. 1983: *Teaching the spoken language*. Cambridge: Cambridge University Press.

*CARTER, R. (ed.) 1982: *Linguistics and the teacher*. London: Routledge & Kegan Paul.

DEPARTMENT OF EDUCATION AND SCIENCE 1975: *A language for life* (The Bullock Report). London: HMSO.

— 1979: *Aspects of secondary education in England*. London: HMSO.

— 1983: *How well can 15-year-olds write?* London: HMSO.

*GANNON, P. and CZERNIEWSKA, P. 1980: *Using linguistics: an educational focus*. London: Edward Arnold.

GOODY, J. 1977: *The domestication of the savage mind*. Cambridge: Cambridge University Press.

HALLIDAY, M.A.K. 1973: *Explorations in the functions of language*. London: Edward Arnold.

HALLIDAY, M.A.K. and HASAN, R. 1976: *Cohesion in English*. London: Longman.

*KEEN, J. 1978: *Teaching English: a linguistic perspective*. London: Methuen.

MALLETT, M. and NEWSOME, B. 1977: *Talking, writing and learning 8–13* (Schools Council Working Paper 59). London: Evans/Methuen.

QUIRK, R., GREENBAUM, S., LEECH, G. and SVARTVIK, J. 1972: *A grammar of contemporary English*. London: Longman.

RICHMOND, J. 1982: *The resources of classroom language*. London: Edward Arnold.

*STUBBS, M. 1980: *Language and literacy*. London: Routledge & Kegan Paul.

*THORNTON, G. 1980: *Teaching writing: the development of written language skills*. London: Edward Arnold.

Readers are recommended to read the published reports of the Assessment of Performance Unit (Language). These are published by the Department of Education and Science, and are available from HMSO and through booksellers. Entitled *Language performance in schools*, they are reports on the language performance of children in England and Wales, at ages 11 and 15 (separate volumes). A description of the Unit's framework of assessment is contained in reports 1 and 2.

DEPARTMENT OF EDUCATION AND SCIENCE 1981: *Language performance in schools. Primary survey report No. 1*. London: HMSO.

— 1982a: *Language performance in schools. Primary survey report No. 2*. London: HMSO.

— 1982b: *Language performance in schools. Secondary survey report No. 1*. London: HMSO.

— 1983: *Language performance in schools. Secondary survey report No. 2*. London: HMSO.

— 1984: *Language performance in schools: 1982 primary survey report*. London: DES.